Gridlock

Dublin's transport crisis and the future of the City

 publications to date

Out of Reach
Inequalities in the Irish Housing System
by PJ Drudy and Michael Punch December 2005

Engaging Citizens
The Report of the Democracy Commission
Edited by Clodagh Harris October 2005

Post Washington
Why America can't rule the World
by Tony Kinsella and Fintan O'Toole June 2005

For Richer, For Poorer
An investigation of the Irish Pension System
by Jim Stewart May 2005

An Outburst Of Frankness
Community arts in Ireland – a reader
edited by Sandy Fitzgerald November 2004

Selling Out?
Privatisation in Ireland
by Paul Sweeney October 2004

After the Ball
by Fintan O'Toole October 2003

 research pamphlets to date

Outsourcing Government
public bodies and accountability
by Paula Clancy and Grainne Murphy

The Trouble with Northern Ireland May 2006
the belfast agreement and democratic governance
by Rick Wilford and Robin Wilson April 2006

tasc

A Think Tank for Action on Social change
26 Sth Frederick St, Dublin 2.
Ph: 00353 1 6169050
Email:contact@tascnet.ie
www.tascnet.ie

Gridlock
Dublin's transport crisis and the future of the City

James Wickham

tasc | at NEW ISLAND

Gridlock
First published 2006
by tasc at New Island
an imprint of New Island Press
2 Brookside
Dundrum
Dublin 14

www.newisland.ie

The author has asserted his moral rights.

ISBN: 1-905494-28-9

Typeset by Ashfield Press
Cover design by Public Communications Centre

Printed in Ireland by
Betaprint Limited, Dublin

Contents

THE AUTHOR

JAMES WICKHAM studied sociology at the London School of Economics and the University of Frankfurt; he took his Ph.D. from the University of Sussex. He has been awarded a Jean Monnet Professorship in European Employment Studies at Trinity College Dublin where he is a Fellow and directs the Employment Research Centre in the School of Social Sciences and Philosophy. He has published in journals such as *Social History, Work Employment and Society, Gender Work & Society, Journal of Education and Work, Innovation, European Journal of Education* and *European Societies*

For Jessica, Lottie and Lorelei – Luas fans all

Acknowledgements

Like Dublin's Luas, this book has been a long time coming. At times progress has been like a fast car in a Bangkok traffic jam: a lot of promise, but going nowhere. It all started because of a conversation with my colleague Hilary Tovey about food chains, canned meat, Argentinian cowboys and technologies that we take for granted. This eventually led to a successful proposal to the European Commission for a study of 'embedded technologies' focusing on the role of the car in European cities.

That research project was formally known by the rather unlovely acronym 'SceneSusTech' with the subtitle 'Scenarios for Sustainable Technology: Car-Systems in the city and the sociology of embedded technologies'[1]. It involved teams from Finland, Italy and Greece, as well as Ireland. Our joint work helped put Dublin's problems in a wider context; many of the arguments in this book were first developed in team meetings across Europe. In particular all of us would thank Professor Marja Javela for her hospitality and intellectual stimulation during a memorable workshop in rural Finland. Back in Brussels Ronan O'Brien at the European Commission encouraged us to develop our ideas and nagged us to deliver research reports – his involvement in the project went well beyond the call of duty and showed that 'Brussels bureaucrats' can have a most unbureaucratic passion for European social research. Meanwhile in Dublin Maria Lohan's commitment kept the project on the rails while she also carried out much of the original Dublin fieldwork.

Maria Lohan wrote up most of the initial Dublin project reports; Piergiulio Poli helped with the analysis of the Dublin expert focus group. Fieldwork and project reports in Athens were carried out by the team led by Kostas Sakellaropoulos (Dimitri Balourdos, Aliki Mouriki, E. Theodoropolos and

Kostos Tsakiris); in Bologna research was by Fatima Farina and Elena Battalgini; in Helsinki by Marja Javela and Tiaina Rajanti. I owe a special debt to Maria Lohan: Chapter 2 develops her original research report on the development of the car system in Dublin and Chapter 4 derives partly from her initial literature review. Of course, only I need take responsibility for the particular interpretation presented here!

After some delay, the final results of the project were written up in 2002. Since that time many people in Ireland and abroad have contributed to the development of that original research into this book about Dublin. I have learnt much from discussions at workshops and seminars organised by, amongst others, the European Conference of Ministers of Transport, the European Commission, the Public Transport Partnership Forum and Engineers Ireland. Colleagues at the Employment Research Centre, in particular Gráinne Collins, have been a sounding board for my ideas. At Trinity College's Policy Institute Bob Holton and Frances Ruane facilitated further research on Dublin – and will in due course be rewarded with a long-promised report on transport and social exclusion.

My thanks also to many who provided information, in particular Carmel McCartney, Catherine Murply, Chris van Egeraat, Christian Schweiger, David Charles, Derek Wheeler, Frank McCabe, Frank McDonald, Gabrielle Breslin, Ger Gibbons, John Henry, Michael Doherty, Robert Watt, Suzanne Harkins and Tom Manning. At tasc Paula Clancy and Phill McCaughey ensured that – much to their surprise – a vague idea finally turned into a real book, while Bernard Feeney, Jeff Kenworthy, Mary Corcoran and Paul Sweeney all read and commented on an initial draft.

JAMES WICKHAM

April 2006

Note

1   Funded by the European Commission within the Targeted Socio-Economic Research (TSER) programme of the Fourth Framework Programme. Contract number: SOE1-CT97-1071. Co-ordinator: James Wickham, Trinity College Dublin.

Introduction

In summer 2004 the Luas opened. By then everyone in Ireland knew that luas, Irish for speed, was the name of the capital city's new tram, the arrival of which had been anything but speedy. Government had first given the go-ahead in 1992, but then spent most of the 1990s prevaricating over its final route. Once construction began the final completion seemed to recede ever further into the future and the project was more and more over budget. Luas became a by-word for chaos and incompetence.

But then suddenly the sun came out. In spring 2004 the trams began trial running on the Sandyford line. Stuck in buses in Harcourt Street, delayed by the still ongoing Luas works, passengers could be heard admiring the shiny new trams as they clanged their way down the new car-free Lána Tram. And by the time Luas opened for business in the summer, Luas seemed to have become more admired as an icon of the new city than the Spire in O'Connell Street.

At the time of writing it is too early to judge how successful Luas itself will be. And certainly not even the two Luas lines will somehow solve Dublin's traffic problem. Yet Luas's transformation from national joke to city symbol has wider implications. It provides a glimpse of Dublin as a city with good public transport – and as a city of which Dubliners could be proud. It shows that choices in urban transport go far beyond issues of how people are to move around. When Dubliners got excited about their new trams, they were actually showing more sense than the cost accountants and economists who dominate so much policy discussion of transport in Ireland – and who have contributed to the disaster of Dublin's traffic.

Proper public transport is essential for Dublin. Traffic jams are a nuisance and impose costs on business; the city's car addiction makes the city environmentally unsustainable. Yet ultimately far more is involved. Public transport is necessary if the people who live in Dublin are to fully become citizens of Dublin, and it is not too exaggerated to say that proper public transport is necessary if Dublin is to be a real capital city for the people of Ireland. This claim involves eight linked arguments, each of which forms a chapter of this book.

Firstly, rising car usage is not an inevitable consequence of rising affluence or economic growth. Bizarrely, given the growing rhetoric of market choice, Dublin has increasingly become a city in which people have no choice but to use a car to participate in normal life, whether this means going to work, shopping, maintaining social links, or just entertainment. In this sense Dublin has become a *car dependent* city.

Secondly, this car dependency has been the result of a series of choices that are ultimately political. In the second half of the 20th century, Dublin's public transport system was destroyed. Even before the boom of the 1990s, the city was becoming more and more suburbanised, and in a way that exacerbated its inhabitants' dependency on the car. With a weak city government, no metropolitan government whatsoever and a central government totally disinterested in urban life, the city was shaped purely by the unco-ordinated interests of property developers. The Celtic Tiger boom has involved two contradictory trends. On the one hand, this developer-led development has accelerated, with Greater Dublin splurging into much of Leinster, as the city becomes an American edge city of car-based suburbs and shopping malls. On the other hand, various interest groups, city officials and intellectuals have begun to formulate and implement an alternative vision of Dublin as a relatively compact and environmentally sustainable European city.

Today transport is one of the battlegrounds of these

two visions. The third chapter assesses the current state of public transport in Dublin today. It shows how, despite the real improvement delivered by Luas, Quality Bus Corridors (QBCs) and strict parking controls, most of the city remains car dependent because of the low quality of public transport, whether measured in terms of users' satisfaction, the ability to innovate or the integration of the network.

Car dependency has negative consequences for the city as a whole. As the fourth chapter shows, a city that depends on cars is a polluting city. Compared with other European cities, Dublin has now become an extreme case of environmentally unsustainable growth.

Fifthly, car dependency is an issue for social policy. Car dependency exacerbates social exclusion, for those who do not have a car run the risk of being excluded from normal life. Their access to jobs is restricted, they find it difficult to move around the city, they are not full citizens.

Yet as the sixth chapter shows, car dependency undermines the quality of life of *all* citizens. It creates private spaces and destroys public space, while public transport potentially creates a collective good and a public resource.

The next chapter argues that quality of public transport is not dependent on private ownership and the market. It is time to be sceptical of private enterprise fanatics who claim that the public sector is inherently inefficient and unable to innovate. Comparative evidence shows that the debate over privatisation is a red herring: where public transport is provided by private companies it is not inevitably better than publicly owned enterprises. Indeed, there is now much evidence the other way round: privatising public transport and expanding competition can often undermine public services.

The final stage of the argument is that achieving effective public transport in Dublin will depend on a powerful city government and on some form of transit authority. Until the city is responsible for its own transport decisions, transport will remain a mess. Rather than asking what the minister is going to do next, we should be asking when he is going to allow Dubliners to decide on Dublin's transport.

The final chapter starts with possible scenarios for the future developed through interviews with experts in four European cities. It goes on to outline a different Dublin: a *multi-modal city* in which citizens have genuine choices as to how they move around and, indeed, as to how they will live. Of course this requires accelerated investment in public transport, and here the proposed rail interconnector turns out to be crucial, but it also requires institutional change and new political coalitions. A decade ago such arguments would have seen utopian. Today there is a growing realisation that change is possible. Hopefully this book will make some small contribution to transforming Dublin from *car city* into a capital city of which its citizens and the entire country can be proud.

Chapter 1

Car city?

Dublin is now a car city. Most households have one car; many households have several. Dubliners use their cars to travel to work, to shop, to visit friends, to go out for the evening. In fact, for most people, normal life without a car would be impossible. Dublin is car dependent.

Does this matter? And even if it matters, can anything be done about it? Until recently everyone but cranks believed that rising car ownership and rising usage were inevitable and indeed desirable, a welcome aspect of growing economic prosperity. From this perspective the solution to traffic jams is simple: build more roads. The role of transport planners is simply to calculate the future levels of car ownership and to ensure that roads are built as quickly as possible to facilitate them. Such a 'predict and provide' philosophy is less respectable than it used to be. It is widely recognized that building more roads just leads to more cars, and hence more traffic jams. More and more people are aware, if only vaguely, that cars are 'bad for the environment'. The car seems at best a very mixed blessing: sometimes a pleasure, sometimes a nuisance, but always a necessity. And as people travel abroad to other cities, they notice that some of them seem to manage things rather better than we do. As we shall now see, other cities are less dependent on the car than Dublin, and this turns out to have little to do with wealth or, more surprisingly, population density.

YOU CAN'T DO WITHOUT THE CAR: DEFINING CAR DEPENDENCY

In Ireland today nearly 80% of all households have at least one car, a proportion that has increased continually for over half a century. Whereas several decades ago it was the 'family' that owned a car, now the car has become much more an individual possession. In any reasonably affluent suburban area of Dublin, there will usually be several cars in the driveway. For example, in South County Dublin, according to the 2002 census, 84.3% of all households had at least one car, and fully 41.7% had two or more cars. Where the household comprises a married couple, husband and wife will usually each have their own car, as may well any young adults still living at home. In future it seems, every adult will have their own car, since already every adult apparently wants their own car.

At one level people are of course 'choosing' to buy cars and to use them. However, these choices can create a situation where the choice *not* to have a car becomes more and more difficult. As cars become more widespread, so more and more activities become based on the assumption that all participants have cars. The obvious example is the suburban shopping mall, but the same applies to the suburban office park. Doing the weekend shopping requires a car, just as going to work every day does. Car dependency does not just mean that people use cars a lot. It means that alternatives to the car do not exist. Daily life is dependent on the car, whether people like it or not. The physical structures in which life is lived have changed: the shopping mall has replaced the corner shop, the railway was long ago abandoned, the motorway has been built, the bus no longer runs. In this situation the term 'choice' becomes rather inappropriate.

As we shall see, Dublin as a whole has not reached this stage yet. There are, however, large areas of suburban

Dublin where you have to have a car to lead a normal life. Car dependency is strikingly like drug dependency. Initially people choose to use drugs – to drink, to smoke, to shoot up. However, as they continue to do this, their body changes, it becomes restructured, it needs the drug, it cannot do without it. Furthermore, the 'need' escalates – the body requires more and more of the drug, while withdrawal becomes more and more difficult with greater physiological as well as psychological problems. The same applies to car addiction. Driving cars gives many people pleasure, a pleasure they would be very unwilling to give up. Yet to concentrate on the pleasure of owning and driving a car is to ignore the way in which many people's existing lifestyle has become impossible without the use of the car. Reducing car dependency means changing lifestyles – and *changing the physical construction of the city*.

Yet it is not self-evident that this is desirable. In a car-based city the car promises freedom and independence for individuals. Why then should car use be restrained? As later chapters will show, car dependency is self-defeating, it is environmentally unsustainable, it exacerbates social inequality and undermines civil society. A common response to such arguments is that the car may well have these unfortunate side effects, but a continual increase in car usage is inevitable. With continuing economic growth, universal adult car ownership is only a matter of time. As societies get richer, so inevitably car ownership and car usage will increase.

IT ALL DEPENDS ON WHERE YOU LIVE: CITIES AND CAR OWNERSHIP

This rigid connection between prosperity and car ownership is in fact a myth. A sensible discussion of transport policy can only begin when the myth is abandoned. The extent to which people own cars, and the extent to which car owners use their cars, both depend on much more than just income. Once we realize the extent of this variation, then we can begin to understand how Dublin in fact is an extreme case of car dependency – with the obvious implication that it could be different.

One way of seeing how car ownership depends on much more than income is in fact to simply look at the contrasts within the area covered by the Dublin Regional Authority (i.e. the four councils of Dublin City, Dun Laoghaire-Rathdown, Fingal, and South Dublin). In the centre of the area, in Dublin City itself, household car ownership is only 58% – the lowest for any county or city in the Republic. At the other extreme, in South Dublin household car ownership is fully 84%, comfortably above the national level of 78%. This is not just to do with income: within *every* occupational group, households are less likely to own a car in Dublin City than are similar people in the country as a whole or in the three Dublin counties. For example, 80% of 'higher professional' households in Dublin City own at least one car, as compared with 93% of such households in the state and fully 96% in South Dublin. At the other end of the scale, only 39% of 'unskilled' households in the City own cars, as compared with 63% in the state and 67% in South Dublin. Figure 1.1 shows the overall picture clearly.

In films set in the USA people spend a lot of time jumping in and out of cars. Unless, of course, the film is a Woody Allen film set in Manhattan, in which case the protagonists usually move around by taxi. Indeed, according to one recent newspaper article, many residents of Manhattan do not even know how to drive a car. Manhattan is after all not only densely populated, its inhabitants have some of the highest incomes in the USA. Some people who have enough income to be able to choose where to live, choose to live in areas where there are plentiful local facilities, including ubiquitous taxis and public transport, such that they need not bother with owning a car for their daily journeys. If they want to use one on holiday, they will simply hire one at their destination. Rich people, in other words, may well choose not to spend their money on owning a car. And even if people do have a car, they may well not use it to travel to work, particularly if the city provides alternative forms of transport. Dublin City shows a weak version of this Manhattan effect, illustrating that car ownership does not automatically rise with income.

Figure 1.1 Household Car Ownership and Occupation: Dublin City and Suburbs 2002

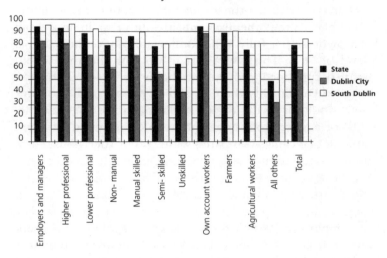

Source: *CSO, Census of Population 2002*

The obvious difference between Dublin City and South County Dublin is population density. Where people live close to each other, and crucially, where people are close to facilities for shopping and entertainment, they have less need of cars. In high-density cities people can make many journeys on foot or on bicycle, and high-density cities are easily served by public transport. Thus US cities (especially those in the West and South West) are built at much lower population densities than European cities, and have correspondingly higher car usage.

The relationship between population density and car usage has been shown by an Australian research team who collected data on transport usage for 37 world cities in 1990 (Kenworthy et al, 1997). The *SceneSusTech* project added to this data set similar information on our four case study cities (Athens, Bologna, Dublin and Helsinki)[1]. Analysis of this data shows exactly what might be expected: there is a straightforward relationship between population density and car ownership, and between population density and the extent to which people use private cars to travel to work. The lower the population density, the more likely people are to own cars, and the more likely they are to use cars to travel to work. At one extreme there are spread-out, low-density American cities such as Los Angeles, with extensive car ownership and almost complete reliance on the car; at the other extreme there are high-density Asian cities such as Tokyo or Singapore, where car ownership is much lower and many people travel to work by public transport.

WEALTH AND CARS

The contrast between Tokyo and Los Angeles immediately alerts us to a fact that is now well established by research. The extent to which people use cars does not depend just on how personally wealthy they are, but on features of the city in which they live. As we have already seen, one simple issue is population density, but another is the quantity and quality of public transport. Indeed, public transport provides the key to what appears, at first, the odd relationship between the wealth of a city and the level of car usage. This is particularly important for Dublin, since it is frequently argued that Dublin's traffic chaos is a result of the Celtic Tiger and rising levels of affluence. Here the fact that our international data stems from the 1990s is actually an advantage, because it allows us to compare Dublin with other cities before the boom of the 1990s.

The scattergram in Figure 1.2 plots all 40 cities on two axes: the vertical axis shows the proportion of journeys to work that are by private car, the horizontal axis the per capita GDP of the region. Thus the higher a city is in the chart, the more journeys are by private car, the further to the right the city, the larger its wealth. If wealth and private car usage were simply related, then the points would be clustered around a diagonal going from the bottom left hand corner of the chart to the top right hand corner (cities which are poor would have low car usage, cities which are rich would have high car usage).

Figure 1.2 Wealth and Journey to Work: 40 Cities

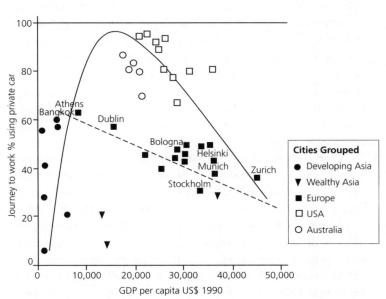

Source: *Kenworthy et al (1997); SceneSusTech*

Certainly car ownership tends to be higher in wealthy cities, but the chart shows clearly that this is not necessarily true for car usage – at least as measured by the mode of travel to work. Across all the 40 cities there is in fact a slightly negative relationship between wealth and the use of private car to travel to work. As Newman and Kenworthy argue, the relationship is really curvilinear: in poor cities car usage is low, as wealth rises so does car usage, but then in the richest cities car usage falls again – as shown by the line linking the cases in the chart.

In fact, if we just examine the 15 European cities on which we have data, there is a simple negative relationship: the richer the city, the *less* people use cars to travel to work. Of the European cities in the 1990s, Athens and Dublin were the two poorest but actually had the highest levels of journey to work by private transport. Thus within the European data there is in fact a *negative* relationship between the extent of car ownership in a city and the extent to which people use their car to travel to work. Car ownership and car usage are very different. In Athens, one of the poorest cities in the data set, anybody who can afford a car buys one and uses it for the basic journeys, since the alternatives are non-existent. By contrast, as Figure 1.3 shows, in Helsinki, Zurich and Bologna more people own cars, but fewer people use them to travel to work.

One reason for this is that rich cities can also choose to spend money collectively, on public transport. Rather than sitting separately in traffic jams, the citizenry decides to spend money on collective transport facilities. This has clearly occurred in some European cities. In Zurich for example (the wealthiest city on Figure 1.2) the city has been continually upgrading its public transport system for more than twenty years, and the key reason has simply been that this improves the quality of life of the citizenry. From this perspective, as cities get richer, they can then afford to spend money on public transport. Because of this collective decision, people are able to spend less time in their cars – in Zurich the proportion of people travelling to work by private car has stayed low for the simple reason that public transport has been continually improved (Apel and Pharaoh, 1995).

Figure 1.3 Car Ownership and Journey to Work: 15 European Cities

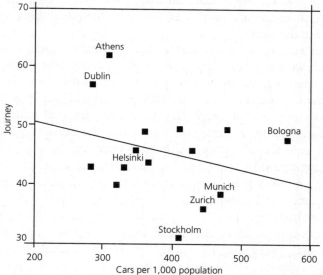

Source: *Kenworthy et al (1997); SceneSusTech*

The relationship between a city's wealth and the extent of car usage also goes the other way round. Where people have to use the car for the most basic journeys, then traffic jams proliferate and mobility slows. This also affects the business environment and makes the city unattractive for new investment. Accordingly, public transport is not just, in economists' jargon, a consumption good, it is also an investment. Cities that invest in public transport are able to attract new investment – and so become even richer.

POPULATION AND PLANNING

Even more surprisingly, the relationship between population density and car usage turns out to be less straightforward than it first appears. As we have seen, low-density
American cities certainly have higher levels of car usage
than more densely populated European cities. However,
this is only true if we compare the USA with Europe as a
whole. Taking the 15 European cities on which we have
data by themselves produces no relationship between density and car usage. Thus Athens has one of the highest population densities in Europe, but also an even higher level of
car usage than Dublin.

Since Athens is so densely populated, one might expect
that people would often walk to work and that, furthermore, its population structure would have facilitated public
transport. However, this has not happened. Until very
recently, public transport in Athens meant taxis, overcrowded and inefficient buses, one metro line and an almost irrelevant railway line. Facilities for cycling and walking are virtually non-existent; cars frequently block pavements and
always pollute the atmosphere, so walking is unpleasant
and even dangerous. In many ways this description of
Athens could be a description of Bangkok, another city that
is notorious the world over for its traffic jams (Kenworthy,
1995; Jenks, 2003). Like Athens, Bangkok invested very little
in public transport in the period of the city's rapid growth
(as Figure 1.2 shows, travel to work by private car in
Bangkok in the early 1990s was nearly as high as in Athens
and higher than Dublin). While its population density
would have made the city highly suitable for public transport, there was no political will to provide it. As a result,
Bangkok and Athens have become cities swamped by the
private car.

At the other extreme, both Dublin and Helsinki have a
population density approximately one seventh of Athens.

Yet although they have almost the same population densities, Dublin and Helsinki are two extreme cases for car usage – very high in Dublin, very low in Helsinki. Helsinki combines low population density and high public transport use because land-use and transport planning are linked. Much suburban housing, suburban employment and suburban shopping facilities are concentrated at public transport nodes, where the metro line links with local bus services. Suburban housing does not in this case always mean suburban sprawl. Similarly in Copenhagen most of the expansion of the city has occurred along transport 'fingers' reaching out from the city, ensuring that both local facilities and the city centre are in easy reach of the suburbs. By contrast in Dublin, as in most American cities, suburban housing and employment sprawl out across the countryside, disconnected from any transport links. Here suburbia is car-based.

In Athens, as in many southern European cities, most of the city comprises closely packed apartment blocks; there are very few owner-occupied single houses as in Northern Europe. As in Dublin, there is no effective land use planning and until very recently, no investment in public transport. Accordingly, Athens' extensive suburbs are car-based, even though they are also (by Northern European standards) high-density. High-density housing by itself is not the 'magic bullet' to replace the car.

HISTORY AND TRAJECTORY

Of course, one difference between Europe and the USA is simply history: European cities are older than their US counterparts. European cities often have historic cores that can only be preserved by radically limiting the motorcar. In this original 'walking city' (Newman and Kenworthy, 1996) most destinations can be reached on foot. However, in most cases such historic centres occupy a very small amount of the total land area of the contemporary city. Within European cities a more important inheritance from the past is that such cities also often have *legacy systems* of public transport. The great metropolises of 19th century Europe were built around a public transport system that was created before the advent of the motorcar. By the 1920s cities such as London, Paris and Berlin had systems of trams, metros and suburban rail that allowed their inhabitants to move easily over a large densely inhabited area. In many ways the inter-war period was the golden age of public transport (Wolf, 1996).

For cities today, the crucial question is what happened to this inheritance. At the beginning of the 20th century, Dublin had some limited suburban rail and above all an extensive tram system. Unlike Helsinki and unlike most German cities, the trams were entirely removed in the 1950s, as was much of the local railway system. Accordingly, Dublin has a very weak legacy system.

Since the oil shocks of the 1970s, the oil-dependence of rich Western societies has increasingly been perceived as a problem. Initially the concern was strategic, interwoven with concern over non-renewable energy. During the 1980s environmental concerns were added to the list, followed in the 1990s by a growing awareness of the negative social consequence of high motorcar usage. Thus, whereas in the 1950s and 1960s the car was unchallenged, it has become problematic. Notoriously, however, such concerns have not prevented the continual expansion of motorcars. Yet once again what this hides is the very different experiences of different countries and even of different cities.

During the last quarter century US cities have become more and more car-based. By contrast, in Europe car ownership has tended to grow more slowly and, especially in the cities, car usage has also grown more slowly. Car ownership and car usage do not increase in a one-to-one relationship with economic growth and to some extent car usage can become *uncoupled* from economic growth. The result is that, although everywhere car travel is increasing, the gaps between countries and above all between cities have been increasing.

The concept of *technological trajectory* in the sociology of technology can be used to explain this. Technological change, so the argument goes, is not random but occurs along a given path – it is 'path dependent'. This is partly a question of ideas and skills (how problems are understood and how they can be solved), but also of interests and even power (participants have built careers by developing particular expertise and knowledge). Applied to transport, this suggests that confronted by a traffic jam, the obvious solution is to build more roads. All sorts of people and all sorts of institutions have an 'interest' in this solution to the problem. Transport planners, motorists lobby groups, construction companies etc. all support the roads solution and all are in turn beneficiaries. Alternative lines of development (e.g. new public transport) become seen as impossible, implausible, impractical, naïve. And this to some extent is true. Those putting forward the alternatives do not have the skills or the resources of their opponents.

However, it is quite clear that 'European' transport solutions are now embedded in European society and are different from American ones. This 'European' trajectory dates in part from the 1970s. That itself shows how trajectories can change, and that it is possible to identify *switching points* where development changes direction. Opposition emerges to the existing trajectory and begins to develop a coherent alternative. New ideas and new skills develop. Equally, new interest groups develop that support and benefit from the new trajectory. Such groups may be new, but it may also be a question of reconfiguring alliances. For example, property developers may start making their profits from developments around transit nodes, and so begin to promote public transport; construction companies begin to develop expertise in transit construction, and so support expansion of the system.

In the 1970s such switching points occurred in some European cities. The continued expansion of car ownership had been seen as inevitable and desirable, but in some cities forces emerged to restrain the car and reinvigorate public transport. In all four of our case study cities during the 1960s, journeys by car begin to replace those on public transport. At the same time, increased car ownership expanded the number of journeys undertaken. Two dramatic responses to this occurred in Helsinki and Bologna.

The city government of Helsinki put forward a plan to redesign the city in the interests of car transportation (the Smith-Polvinen plan), proposing urban motorways and a quadrupling of parking spaces in the city centre. This created considerable public debate. Ultimately the city was forced to abandon the plan and instead begin construction of a metro; a new consensus emerged that, at least in the city centre, the car should be restrained.

In Bologna the apparently unceasing rise of the car (by the 1960s the Piazza Maggiore was used as a car park) threatened to completely swamp the city. The Bologna city administration began work on its radical traffic plan in 1972. The plan, finally accepted in 1974, was probably the most radical transport policy in Europe – its prioritisation of public transport even included free fares for rush-hour journeys (Jaggi et al, 1977).

The new policy in favour of public transport was originally very controversial. In both Helsinki and Bologna the political parties divided on left-right lines. In Bologna the plan to promote public transport was a policy of the PCI that met opposition from right wing parties; in Helsinki the Social Democratic party's plan for a new metro was its most controversial decision of the period. However, this new policy direction did not remain controversial. In both cities in subsequent years most political parties and many business enterprises and organisations came to accept a greater role for public transport and restrictions on private cars.

By contrast, road building continued in Athens and Dublin, delayed sometimes by bureaucratic inertia but never by any alternative policy or vision. The early 1970s was therefore a historic turning point: in Bologna and Helsinki a new political consensus was created which accepted limiting the private car as a policy objective, something that did not happen in Dublin.

CONCLUSION: DUBLIN AT THE CROSSROADS?

Thirty years later, it is Dublin that faces a possible switching point. There is widespread awareness that simply building more roads is no solution and quite extensive support for improved public transport. Interwoven with this, city planners in particular have developed and even implemented ambitious plans to regenerate the city centre, based on a vision of Dublin as an attractive 'European' city. At the same time, however, the city's commuter belt now includes much of Leinster, motorway building is accelerating and with it the increasing suburbanisation of shopping and employment, all far from any public transport. American-style suburbia surrounds and perhaps will soon swamp the tentatively Europeanised city centre.

Turning Dublin into a city in which car dependency is controlled depends on three clear things. First of all, the *box* – the framework of land use planning that reduces the overall need for journeys and which ensures that 'traffic generators' such as workplaces are located near public transport. Secondly, the *sticks* – measures that manage the demand for car travel by traffic calming, parking controls and road pricing. And finally, the *carrot* – a public transport *system* that people can use. The role of such a system and how it can be created is the central topic of this book.

Note:
1   See Appendix for a summary of the research project methodology.

Chapter 2

Building the car into the city

How has it come about that Dublin is so dominated by the private car? Comparing Dublin with other cities has shown that Dublin is a relatively extreme case of car usage. Economic growth has simply pushed Dublin even faster down the road to a car-based city – *probably faster than the same level of growth would have done in other cities.* Once this trajectory is seen as only one from a range of possibilities, we then have to ask how this trajectory has come about. What are the ideas, politics and interests that are responsible for this *technological lock-in?*

Part of the answer is to do with history and culture. It is about how Dublin has been constituted within Irish history, and about the role of politics and the political system. This is interwoven with the development of the physical infrastructure of the city, above all the rapid destruction in the 20th century of key elements of its public transport system. Politics and infrastructure in turn are both cause and effect of the massive suburbanisation of Dublin in the last forty years, for while suburbanisation is a general feature of all European cities, Dublin is an extreme case. In the last ten years, new ideas of the city have emerged, contributing to the rebuilding of parts of the inner city but unable to develop enough impetus to halt the consolidation of the car-based city region.

THE CITY IN THE NATION

In 1800 Dublin was one of the largest cities in the then United Kingdom. The beauty and the novelty of its architecture and town planning reminded observers of St Petersburg. Yet while St Petersburg was the result of despotic planning, Dublin's elegant squares essentially stemmed from free-market speculative building. Nonetheless, the speculators managed to combine profit and inspired aesthetics in a manner that their contemporary successors unfortunately do not emulate. Equally, they created public spaces instead of destroying them. Finally, the great public buildings – the Customs House, the Four Courts, the City Hall and Mansion House – all remain city landmarks, setting a standard that the architect Sam Stephenson was to consciously try to emulate in the dark days of the 1970s and 1980s with the new Civic Offices and Central Bank.

However, the problem was of course that Dublin was also a colonial city. In the 18th century social inequality in Dublin was extreme even by the standards of the time – another way in which Dublin was compared to St Petersburg. Dublin was not just the administrative centre of British rule; it was also the social and political centre of the Anglo-Irish ascendancy. It is therefore somewhat bizarre that conventional nationalist history used to complain that the Act of Union was responsible for much of the landlord class absenting themselves to England! In fact, the decline of Georgian Dublin has probably more to do with Dublin's first suburbanisation, the migration of the affluent to the southern townships along the coast. As manufacturing industry grew in Britain, and as Irish agriculture was increasingly unable to compete with the New World produce, Dublin's decline within the 19th century UK was assured.

By 1900 Dublin had become smaller than many English and Scottish cities; within Ireland it was an economic backwater compared with Belfast. In the new industrial cities of

Victorian Britain, new urban elites set about, in the words of their recent historian Tristram Hunt, 'Building Jerusalem' (Hunt, 2004). For them, the city was to be transformed from a *dystopia* of urban squalor and anomie into a new, self-governing entity, combining economic dynamism with intellectual enlightenment and cultural munificence. This middle class vision of the city was shared by the good Protestant grandees of Belfast – as evidenced by the splendour of Belfast City Hall. Continental European cities of the 19th century were usually refashioned in more authoritarian ways, with Haussmann's famous boulevards slicing through working class Paris to create the global city of the epoch. And such 'bourgeois' urban visions could morph into municipal socialism, as in early 20th century Glasgow ('Red Clydeside') or the Webbs' reformist London County Council. This urban tradition reached its apogee in 'Red Vienna' of the 1920s and early 1930s. Under social democratic rule, the Austrian capital was known across Europe not only for its extensive social welfare system; its cultural programmes and, above all, housing programmes attempted to create a new urban lifestyle for its supporters.

All such ideologies had rather different visions of the city, but they all shared a fundamental belief in the validity of the city. They were all committed to political initiative and urban improvement; they all tended to stress the importance of urban self-government and the active political engagement of the citizenry.

Dublin (but not Belfast) largely missed out on such developments. The reason was not simply economic stagnation, but the control of the city by a narrow and short-sighted political leadership dominated by publicans and shopkeepers (Lohan, 1999). Such people were precisely those who had ruled English cities such as Manchester and Birmingham in the early 19th century, and who were replaced by municipal reformers such as Joseph Chamberlain. In Dublin there were certainly some forces of urban renewal. There were elite social reformers, the 'urban gentry' such as the founders of the Statistical and Social Inquiry Society. There was a remarkably cosmopolitan bohemian intelligentsia, while later Dublin Labour too focused on municipal reform. Yet these forces had only marginal influence on the physical structure of the city itself.

After the achievement of political independence, the city became intellectually marginal to the new nation. For the new nationalist elite Georgian Dublin, just like the Big Houses of the countryside, was quite simply part of the previous regime. It should be neglected or, even better, actually destroyed. Like the Ayatollahs of present day Iran, who at times want to eradicate the remains of the palace of Persepolis (dating from the 6th century BC) because it alerts Iranians to their pre-Islamic past (de Bellaigue, 2005), nationalists ensured that until the 1970s virtually no attempt was made to make Dublin part of a new national culture.

Ireland was hardly unique in that its intellectuals discovered that its true language, its true music, its true culture, all resided outside the city. However, Irish ruralism does seem to have been particularly pronounced, so that for much of the 20th century the real Ireland apparently resided somewhere to the west of the Aran Islands. Conversely, Dublin seemed to lie at the centre of the Pale – an alien incursion into the body of the nation. And if the first edition of Maurice Craig's classic history of Dublin architecture describes the city's heritage crumbling from neglect (Craig, 1952), by the 1970s it was being actively demolished. The city expanded in the 1970s, but every weekend young civil servants headed home to the country to where the action (and their GAA team) was. By contrast, in the rest of Europe the flow was the other way round, as at the weekends young people went 'up' to the city for the excitement of the bright lights.

Other countries' history shows that there was nothing inevitable about this ejection of the capital city from the nation. Finland became independent at almost exactly the same time as Ireland. Finnish nationalism is interwoven with ruralism: the National Gallery of Finland is full of paintings of real Finnish peasants; Sibelius, the composer of the national anthem, filled his music with peasant motifs. Yet crucial also to Finnish national identity is Helsinki, in which the modern buildings from the 1920s, built in a self-consciously 'Finnish' style, proclaim this the capital of the new state. And this even though Helsinki too was in origin 'foreign' and today is still partly Swedish speaking.

All over Europe, new states have appropriated a different past into a national tradition. Thus one of the showpieces of modern Polish heritage is the old city of Gdansk, otherwise known as Danzig, once a (German) Hanseatic League city. The Soviet Union certainly demolished churches and cathedrals, but also turned the Tsars' imperial palaces into museums of the People. In Ireland by contrast, it was possible as late as 1966 for Nelson's column in O'Connell Street to be blown up by 'republicans' and in the 1970s a few young national socialists even lost their political virginity by destroying the elegant monument to Queen Victoria's visit in Dun Laoghaire. If the city's past was seen as alien to the national present, it was hardly surprising that the independence of Ireland meant the destruction of Dublin. The cultural context contributed to the city's political weakness. Conversely, the city's tentative renaissance today is indicated by the fact that the Victoria memorial has been rebuilt and Nelson's pillar replaced by the Spire.

One cause of Dublin's weakness has therefore been a specific animus against the city by the political elite. This is often strengthened by popular resentment against Dublin's dominance of the rest of the country: Dublin's relative size means that it seems to overshadow everything else. However, as the example of Helsinki shows yet again, such a demographic dominance need not produce hostility from the rest of the country. There is no inherent reason why Dublin should not be a capital city of which all the nation's citizens are proud.

RISE AND DECLINE OF PUBLIC TRANSPORT

The relationship between the form of the city and transport can be seen simply as involving three historical stages. Until the 19th century, the normal city is a 'walking city' that can essentially be traversed on foot, or if that is not possible, people can go about their daily activities within their locality without any mechanical transport. In the 19th century the development of omnibuses, trams and suburban rail, as well as underground railways in some cities, allows the creation of 'transit cities' with inner tram-based suburbs and outer rail-based suburbs on rail corridors. From the 1940s onwards there is the emergence of the 'car city' where most areas can normally only be reached by private car (Newman and Kenworthy, 1996).

This three-stage model requires some modification. At least within Europe, mechanised mobility in the city had two different dimensions. Firstly, public transport enabled people to travel from the suburbs to the city centre, especially for the daily commuting journey from home to work. For these journeys suburban railways were decisive. They allowed an enormous expansion of the physical area of the city and, especially for the new middle classes, the separation of work and home into totally distinct districts. This was the new *transit city*. At the same time, much less studied but probably affecting more people, there was the expansion of relatively short-range mobility. For these journeys the tram and, in the very big cities, the metros were decisive, even though these same modes of transport were also used for longer commuting journeys. In particular this mechanisation of mobility expanded the city centre, so that by the start of the 20th century public transport enabled the urban population to criss-cross the city centre using short-haul public transport. This expanded the area that people could reach as if they were on foot, so that these cities were not just transit cities but also what could be called *pavement cities*.

By contrast today all cities are, to some extent, 'car cities', but Chapter 1 has shown that there is considerable variation. There is no historical law that every city must become as car dependent as Los Angeles. This is partly because of the different relationships between the historical 'transit city' and the contemporary 'car city'. Two issues are involved here: firstly, the extent to which the new car city has expanded beyond the earlier transit city and secondly, the extent to which older forms of transport remained viable or even contracted during the second half of the 20th century. Here in fact lies one basis for Dublin's extreme car dependency: the extent to which the infrastructure of both the transit city and the pavement city was destroyed from the 1920s onwards. By the 1950s this had cleared the way for the car-based city and crucially, for a widening gap in car usage between Dublin and many other European cities. The basis for the car-dependent expansion of the 1990s was laid by the 1950s.

Transit city and pavement city

The railway line between Dun Laoghaire (then Kingstown) and Dublin city was originally planned to transfer goods and mail between Dun Laoghaire harbour and Dublin City. However, from its opening in 1834 it carried passengers and intermediate stations were soon built along the route (Merrion, Booterstown, Blackrock and Salthill), enabling the expansion of the city southwards along the coast of Dublin Bay. Indeed, the line has been claimed as the world's first suburban railway. Although Dublin soon became the centre of the national railway network, all the main lines not only ended at different termini – a consequence of their construction by different private companies – they also functioned to only a limited extent as suburban lines. Apart from the extension to Howth, there was no dedicated suburban line to the north of the city; there was little suburban traffic on the lines to Broadstone or Kingsbridge (today's Heuston). Of later lines, the only real suburban line was the Harcourt Street line (the Dublin and South-Eastern Railway), significantly built to serve a rather similar public to that served by the original Kingstown railway. Overall, it would seem that the railways contributed relatively little to Dublin's 19th century growth (McManus, 2002: 310).

Far more important for most Dubliners was the city's tram system. Public transport within the city had originally started as a horse-drawn omnibus system. This was converted to horse drawn tram in 1872 and completely electrified by 1901. The system was continually expanded until World War I, serving most of the inner suburbs and including a radial route from Kenilworth Road to Lansdowne Road. Indeed, Dublin's tram system was seen as one of the most modern and efficient in Europe (e.g. Baker, 1972: 147). Nonetheless, as with the railways, the tram system (and the subsequent bus system) seems to have followed the expansion of the city rather than contributing directly to it (McManus, 2002: 456).

For all the notorious poverty of the inner city, by 1914 Dublin was not only a 'transit city' but also a compact 'pavement city' relatively well served by public transport. As readers of Joyce's Ulysses will realise, it was a city in which its inhabitants could easily move around for work, socialising and pleasure.

Undermining the pavement city: The destruction of urban transport

Within the boundaries of the 1914 transit city, today's Dubliner can move around with greater difficulty than nearly one hundred years ago, unless of course he or she is prepared to take a taxi or use a private car. The key here is the destruction of the tram system, reducing the possibility of commuting by public transport from the inner suburbs and above all, almost completely destroying Dublin as a pavement city.

Today it is all too easy to accept the triumph of the automobile as inevitable, the 'natural' result of a superior technology. There are two rather more critical perspectives on the rise of the private car. Firstly, it can be pointed out that particular interests benefit from particular technological options: at its simplest, car manufacturers and distributors benefit from a switch from public to private transport. Secondly, the private car can be seen as central to a particular stage of capitalism. Writing from his prison cell in the 1920s, the Italian Marxist Antonio Gramsci formulated the term 'fordism' to describe the interlinkage of the new methods of production epitomised by Detroit and the assembly line with new forms of 'mass consumption'. However, neither perspective explains the precise mechanisms whereby these changes occurred, and hence cannot answer the point raised by the radical American historian Yago that 'although automobile transportation is ubiquitous ... patterns of mass transit decline are by no means uniform' (1984: 3).

In one sense the Americanisation of Dublin began in the 1920s. At that time most American cities had excellent transit systems. For example Los Angeles, today seen as the car city par excellence, then had in Pacific Electric one of the most extensive and modern suburban rail systems in the world. Within ten years this system had been systematically destroyed and the construction of the freeway system begun (Bratzel, 1995). This change was hardly inevitable. In some cities in the USA the 1920s saw increased public transport ridership (as in Europe), even though the motorcar was becoming a mass consumption good for the first time. In the first instance the decline of transit was the result of something very close to conspiracy. All across the USA, a coalition of business interests centring on the new auto industries (the car companies, tyre companies, oil interests) bought up the privately owned transit companies and quite literally paved them over with asphalt (Yago, 1984). A process that today appears 'natural' and 'inevitable' was the subject of FBI investigations and even a Congressional inquiry.

More generally, Yago also argued that the decline of transit involved basic transformations of class relationships and was part of the process whereby new economic interest groups, above all of course those of the motor industry itself, began to shape American society. By destroying the rail systems business interests were able to move away from reliance on technologies controlled by strong labour unions; by abandoning transit as an area of investment they were able to move away from an area that had been marked by strong public regulation and consumer movements.

Rather similar processes occurred in Dublin. Facing increased competition from private bus companies in the 1920s, the Dublin tram company first of all bought them up and then used the 1932 Road Transport Act and subsequent legislation to create a monopoly (intriguingly, this is the legal basis now being used to licence competitors for Dublin Bus). Having established its monopoly, the company then set about replacing its tramway lines with bus routes. Initially the technological transfer was successful as bus passenger numbers increased continually. From about 1955, however, bus passenger numbers began to decline, despite the continual growth of the city's population. Soon bus transport entered a vicious circle of falling numbers, falling frequencies and increasingly unreliable service. The bus became a mode of transport people only used if they had no alternative.

Public transport declined in nearly all European cities from the 1950s. However, in many other cities the decline took a different form, often leaving more favourable legacies for a later revival. The key appears to be that in the crucial inter-war period Dublin public transport was in fact privately owned. Dublin's weak municipal traditions ensured that there was never a movement to take public transport in the city into public ownership, as had happened to many tramways elsewhere in Europe. Instead buses and trams in the city were first amalgamated with the railways through the creation of CIÉ as the national transport company in 1944 (Baker, 1972: 119); Dublin transport entered public ownership as part of this *national* company when CIÉ itself was nationalised in 1949, (Baker, 1972: 143).

The contrast with Continental Europe is instructive. For example, in Helsinki the trams began as a private company, but were municipalized in 1913. In German cities such as Frankfurt the trams were usually municipally owned, and in the inter-war period this meant that tramlines were extended out to the new state-built housing areas. In German cities the existing tram systems were rebuilt after World War II; trams were also kept in cities such as Brussels, Helsinki and Milan. Compared with elsewhere in Europe, Dublin's trams were removed remarkably early.

When in the 1970s some European cities began to reinvigorate their urban transit systems, the existing 'old fashioned' trams were a *legacy system* that could be re-used or recycled. The apparent disadvantage of the tram – its restriction to its physical rails – became an advantage. Trams were recognised as more comfortable than buses (transport researchers now estimate that merely replacing buses with trams will itself increase passenger numbers). Their tracks became appreciated as physically linking together the inner area of the city, so that inner city tram-lines were, as in Helsinki, one factor that contributed to the revival of the city centre as an attractive area to live. Equally, whereas trams had been seen by the Dublin 1925 Civic Survey as an 'interference' to road users, from the 1970s it began to be appreciated that their tracks could be used to enforce a new priority for public over private transport within the urban area. Part of the modernisation of Europe's tram systems was the reservation of road space for trams; alternatively tram tracks were put into tunnels and linked to new metro systems. None of this could happen in Dublin. The destruction of the tram system therefore was both cause and effect of an unbundling of the old transit city core, making it more difficult to traverse, and ensuring that no legacy system was available for reinvigoration from the 1970s onwards.

Dublin's limited suburban rail lines were also more run down than lines in many other cities. They had never formed anything that could be termed a railway 'network' and even before car ownership was widespread they suffered from competition from more modern forms of public transport. By the 1920s the DS&ER Harcourt Street Line was already losing traffic to the trams, and by the late 1940s the trams in turn were being replaced by new double-decker buses and the railways also lost more customers (Baker, 1972: 43f, 128). Overall under-investment meant that Dublin's suburban railways were archaic by the time of their demise (in 1948 the *average* age of locomotives owned by the newly formed CIÉ was fully 51 years). The situation was summed up by the nickname for DS&ER line to Bray: 'Damn Slow and Easy Railway'.

By the 1950s the suburban lines were in direct competition with the private car since they served the wealthier suburbs where car ownership was highest. Paradoxically, limited economic growth in Dublin meant that motorcar ownership was not so widespread as elsewhere and it was sometime before car ownership became self-defeating. Photographs of the city in the 1950s show relatively few cars on the streets, and although 'serious traffic congestion' was noted in some streets in Dublin by 1956 (Baker, 1972: 183), it was only in the 1960s that traffic congestion became defined as a general problem. The car remained a realistic and attractive option for Dublin's relatively few middle class commuters for longer than elsewhere.

In this situation the arteries of Dublin's outer transit suburbs were simply severed. Broadstone station on the north of the city had never really had any suburban traffic; the station was closed in the 1930s and eventually became a bus depot (Craig, 1980: 301; Baker, 1972). By 1950 every local railway station within County Dublin on the routes to the west and the south west of the city had been closed; the Harcourt Street Line was closed completely in 1958; services to Bray were reduced in 1960 (Killen, 1992:313).

As with the trams, this destruction ensured that Dublin entered the final quarter of the 20th century without 'heavy rail' being a useful legacy system. A railway company, which was starved of investment, whose management saw its task as managing decline and where employment had become a state-protected sinecure, was unlikely to be able to develop new uses for the remaining tracks. Indeed, almost the only benefit of the company's lack of initiative was that the disused rail bed was simply abandoned rather than sold for any commercial gain.

Stuttering revival: DART and ARROW

Twenty years later all this appeared to be reversed. In 1979, the government gave the go-ahead for the electrification of the coastal railway from Howth to Bray to create the DART. The full title of the DART – Dublin Area Rapid Transit – gives the game away, for electrifying one railway line hardly creates rapid transit for the Dublin Area. What became the

DART line was in fact only one element of proposals for suburban rail *systems* from two studies of the 1970s – the 1971 Dublin Transportation Study and CIÉ's own Dublin Rapid Rail Transport Study of 1975. Rather than developing any coherent transport *policy* for Dublin, the government of the time simply cherry-picked the easiest element of these plans in order to access some of the first EU-funding available for infrastructure in Ireland. While Dublin's population continued to grow, by 1990 total further investment in rail comprised only a cobbled together suburban rail service on the existing Maynooth line (some diesel railcars, the ARROW 'brand name' and four new minimalist stations to serve new housing areas on the line). Neither DART nor ARROW were well integrated with bus services, nor did they presage any change to Irish Rail's well-developed customer-hostility.

Bemoaned by many economists as an extravagance at the time, the DART was nonetheless successful in reversing the trend to car commuting along the coastal corridor. It confirmed the conventional wisdom of transport studies that the best way to achieve a substantial 'modal shift' from private to public transport is precisely such 'heavy rail' in affluent commuter areas. DART was thus the first move to reverse the decay of the city's transit, but at the same time undoubtedly also represented (and still does represent) a subsidy to more affluent commuters. This 'egalitarian' point has often been used to criticise such public expenditure by Irish economists not otherwise known for their commitment to social justice. Such arguments ignore that what is actually needed to tackle inequality is not less public transport, *but more*. In car dependent cities like Dublin or Athens, subsidised public transport involves prestige projects that predominantly benefit isolated groups of well-off commuters. To contribute to social inclusion, public transport has to form a system that is of use to all citizens, and DART was certainly not that. Nonetheless, DART showed that renovated public transport could have a role in Dublin, and more frustratingly, hinted at the possibilities foreclosed by the previous destruction of so much of the city's public transit infrastructure.

Road building: putting the car into Ireland

The car is now so much part of our everyday lives that it is often difficult to see the particular ways in which it enters into and transforms a society. Historians and sociologists of technology argue that new technologies are not simply accepted or 'taken up' by individual consumers. Instead they argue that social processes are involved in which the consumers themselves play an active role: scholars use terms like 'internalise', but also 'normalise', 'interpret', 'domesticate' or even 'shape' to describe this process.

Yet the car seems to escape this analysis. The contrast with the railway is instructive, since in the 19th century railways were widely seen to have transformed society. The railways hardly happened by accident: the railway age rested on great engineering works which are still famous today. The social and environmental impact of the car in the 20th century has been far greater, but much less studied. Part of the reason is that the car, unlike the train, is an individual commodity for purchase by an individual consumer. Any one specific car requires no particular infrastructure, and the use of the car appears not necessarily to involve extensive public works, simply (or at least initially) the piecemeal 'improvement' of existing roads. Unlike the railway, the car enters quietly.

Yet sociologists of technology point out that the car is part of a set of networks (Sorensen and Sorgaard, 1994). Most obviously, cars involve roads, taking up an ever-greater proportion of land, and on a scale never even approached by the construction of railway termini in European cities in the 19th century. Roads require road construction companies, engineers, traffic planners, etc. Cars not only require a car industry to manufacture them, they cannot function without a fuel supply system, workshops for maintenance and repair, let alone the sundry enterprises and occupations involved dealing with car purchase, car taxation, car accidents and car insurance. Less tangibly, but equally essential, there are the specialised skills of everyday car drivers and car users (how to drive a car, follow rules of the road, etc.). In other words, the use of the car involves artefacts, technologies, knowledge and economic interests. Asking how the car entered a society thus involves asking how such a *car system* was created. It involves asking how interest groups develop which promote and normalise the car, campaigning for its appropriate environment (above all the construction of roads), and for the 'rights' of the motorist as a consumer, and generally achieve the *motorisation* of the society.

Such motorisation of the USA involved the activities of major economic interest groups, not least to create the new market, for as Gramsci realised, the mass production of the automobile involved new mass consumption markets. As Henry Ford himself claimed:

'The time will not be far when our very own workers will buy automobiles from us ... I'm not saying our workers will sing Caruso or govern the state. No, we can leave such ravings to the European socialists. But the workers *will* buy automobiles' (quoted Wolf, 1996: 72).

In the USA, as the destruction of public transit showed, coalitions of powerful private economic interests were crucial to the rise of the private car. Within Europe, Nazi Germany was almost the extreme opposite case, where mass consumption of the private car was promoted by the state, not just through the construction of the autobahns, but also through tax incentives for the purchase and use of the private car.

However, Nazi Germany did not achieve mass motorisation: the Volkswagen was planned as the car of the Nazi *Volk*, but was only put into production after the regime collapsed. In fact within Europe it was Britain – or rather southern England – that was motorised first. The car became part of mass consumption in the process whereby the British economy restructured away from the old heavy industries. This was not the England of mass unemployment, hunger marches and the Jarrow Crusade, but the England of the new car factories of Birmingham and Coventry, London's Great West Road and the seaside holiday traffic jam.

In smaller European countries domestication was not automatic either. For example, in Norway the car was resisted until the end of import restrictions in 1960; only during the 1960s did mass motorisation become institutionalised, initially because of active campaigning by government engineers, economists and finally traffic engineers (Østby, 1994). In Ireland until the 1960s, neither private sector interest groups nor the state itself had any commitment to mass motorisation, which anyway seemed precluded by the overall low standard of living. Before the foundation of the state, 'motoring' had been promoted by aristocratic enthusiasts organised in the Royal Irish Automobile Club, yet in the Irish political context these were hardly the most appropriate popularisers of new forms of transport.

There were other isolated sources of support, including the Ford motor company itself, which had opened its first overseas plant in Cork before World War I (Jacobson, 1977). Tariff protection in the 1930s forced motorcar distributors to become unwilling manufacturers, thus creating well-paid workers who also had an interest in an expanding car market. Yet it was these workers rather than the entrepreneurs themselves who campaigned for the retention of tariffs. While workers lost their jobs from the shift to direct imports in the 1960s, the owners were able to move into distribution and expand. Thus the rather inappropriately named Society of the Irish Motor Industry (SIMI) cam-paigned for road building to allow greater use of the private car. By the 1970s construction companies began to realise the profitable potential of road construction, while new professional groups such as engineers and planners became promoters of the continual expansion of road space.

Yet what is striking about Ireland is the *low* physical provision for the car until the 1990s. In the Dublin area the run-down of public transport did not coincide with any extensive or systematic road-building programme. From the 1920s through until the 1970s there were isolated road improvements in the Dublin area. The middle class got some of the earliest accoutrements of car suburbs (a dual carriageway in Foxrock, the later Belfield by-pass) and there were improvements on the radial routes into the city, such as the Naas Road and the Longmile Road. The Myles Wright plan of 1965 and the Dublin Transport Study of 1970 both proposed a motorway ring and an inner tangent road in line with planning orthodoxy of the time, but equal-ly both were delayed by planning appeals and bureaucratic inertia. Eventually the Inner Tangent was simply aban-doned, but not because of any general political revolt of the sort that had stymied such plans in Bologna or Helsinki.

In one sense motorisation in Dublin has been much closer to the experience of Athens or developing Third World cities such as Bangkok than to that of Los Angeles. In Bangkok rapid urbanisation has occurred in the age of the motorcar, not as in European cities in the age of mass transit. Couple this with ineffective urban government and the result is poor public transport in a period when cheap private cars are relatively available. Consequently, public transport soon becomes sitting in a bus in a traffic jam. In this context, everyone buys a car as soon as they can afford it, thus of course creating even more massive traffic jams but also creating popular pressure for improved roads. These cities have not had the experience that improved roads will simply generate more traffic jams, for they have had no extensive road building programmes. Consequently, road building as a solution to traffic appears rational and has both professional and popular support that is lacking in more 'experienced' cities. For example, when the SceneSusTech research team asked traffic experts in Athens, Bologna, Dublin and Helsinki what technologies were needed to improve mobility in their cities, only in Athens was their any support for new roads (Chapter 9).

Suburbanisation and urban non-planning

During the 20th century all cities in the developed world became more suburban, but within Europe Dublin is an extreme case. Furthermore, as Chapter 1 has already shown, even low-density cities within Europe do not necessarily have low public transport use. Helsinki or Copenhagen have become low-density cities, but retain relatively high levels of public transport use, partly because suburban development has occurred around public transport nodes. Dublin's combination of suburbanisation and low public transport usage has to be explained, not just assumed to be an inevitable 20th century fact of life.

Until the 1970s the main driver of suburbanisation in Dublin was state housing policy, with private property developers playing an important but subordinate role. This shows that any simple division into 'bad' private developers and 'good' public development is misleading. Since the 1970s Dublin's suburbanisation has been driven almost entirely by private property developers, initially in housing but spreading quickly into retail and industrial property. In both periods suburbanisation has been totally disconnected from any public transport provision. Although public plans have been plentiful, planning has now become a fig leaf for developer-led development.

Sprawl begins

Up until the mid-1920s the population of the inner city (Dublin between the canals) continued to increase, but thereafter it declined continuously until nearly the end of the century. Whereas in 1926 the inner city population was over quarter of a million, by 1986 it had fallen to less than one third of this. The depopulation of the central city was a key feature of Dublin in the 20th century.

Despite the slow economic growth of the country as a whole, by the 1970s Dublin had spread well beyond the transit city of the early 20th century. The inner suburbs of the late 19th century had been linked to the city centre by tram and later by bus. In late 19th-century Drumcondra, a selling point for new houses was the closeness to the tram (McManus, 2002: 310), while on the south of the city the tram lines usually reached to the end of the built up area. From the 1920s onwards, however, the more expensive private built suburban houses increasingly were equipped with their own garage and accessibility by tram or bus became less important. The 1930s saw a housing boom and the construction of new suburban 'estates', all built at a significantly lower density which would make them less suited to public transport. Nonetheless, in 1935 a builder at the new up-market estate at Mount Merrion was offering to drive potential purchasers to the estate (McManus, 2002: 382), suggesting that car ownership or even car access was still not universal amongst prospective buyers.

The middle class continued to move out from the inner city into new housing in what are today the inner suburbs such as Clontarf and Glasnevin in the north and Rathfarnham and Blackrock in the south. Especially from the 1950s, owner-occupiers left older buildings in areas such as Rathmines so that areas of the Victorian city became private lodgings and bedsits. Middle class housing in Dublin now meant a suburban house, usually with a garage. The city had spread beyond the transit city of the 19th century, making movement without a car difficult but not yet impossible (most housing was still in reach of bus routes).

In the 1960s facilities such as private schools began to follow the move to the suburbs (Alexandra College moved from St. Stephen's Green to its site in what is now the inner suburb of Milltown). When most of UCD moved from Earlsfort Terrace to its suburban campus, the city centre lost the chance of having a real 'left bank' student quarter linking the two main universities. The 1960s also saw shopping centres in the suburbs: Ireland's first opened in Stillorgan in 1966.

For most of the 20th century, however, it was public housing policy that was the major cause of the suburbanisation of the city. To the extent that Dublin was an issue in national politics, it was in terms of its notorious inner city slums. Fianna Fáil's populist politics rested in part on tackling the housing crisis. When the Corporation did build flats within the city in the 1930s, its planning was much influenced by Continental municipal housing programmes such as those in Vienna and (especially) Amsterdam (McManus, 2002: 178). Increasingly, however, housing policy meant decanting as much of the inner city population as possible into 'proper homes'. And with a few limited exceptions, proper homes meant houses with front and back gardens. Public housing was thus primarily large-scale suburban housing, starting with Dublin Corporation's first garden suburb at Marino in the 1920s and reaching its initial peak in Crumlin in the late 1930s. There was of course no railway to Crumlin, and not even a tram. Far more so than in Continental Europe, Dublin's public housing disconnected its inhabitants from the rest of the city.

This policy was accelerated in the 1960s. The Myles Wright *Dublin Region* report advocated building four new towns to the west of the city. These were seen as largely self-contained, each with extensive facilities and local employment. To the extent that these were actually built, they were initially more of the same: large tracts of single class housing with virtually no facilities and often far away from any jobs. In the 1960s there was also a brief flirtation with high-rise developments, most notoriously in Ballymun. Arguably the Ballymun flats were actually superior in layout and design to the standard issue terrace housing. However, partly because the project quickly became a dumping ground for those who needed rehousing quickly, it soon became a social problem in its own right, 'proving' that Irish people could only live happily in low-rise housing. Apart from its tower blocks, Ballymun had much in common with the low-rise estates: extreme social segregation, minimal facilities, almost no small scale retail activity (apart from illegal drugs), and above all, little nearby employment.

In retrospect the public housing of this period seems to have been created with almost no consideration of how people were supposed to earn money. Until the 1970s much employment remained in the city centre, which without a car could only be reached by a long and tortuous bus journey – not a single new housing area had a rail link. Furthermore, although many families could not afford a car, from the 1950s onwards the roads and public spaces are all laid out as if every household was fully motorised. Still today journeys on foot in these areas are long and unpleasant, for pavements and pathways hardly exist. Accordingly, going shopping or going to the pub become major expeditions. By the end of the 1970s Dublin's public housing policy had effectively created car dependency, since the new estates ensured that if the inhabitants were to participate in society they needed to own a car.

Private suburbanisation from 1970s onwards
Almost imperceptibly since the 1970s the Irish state has moved to a minimalist role in housing provision (Drudy and Punch, 2005). This has been particularly important in

Dublin, since the capital had a larger proportion of state housing than elsewhere. The number of new housing units directly built by local authorities has declined, while at the same time existing tenants have been allowed to purchase their housing. This has ensured that local authority housing has increasingly become housing of last resort. In the absence of any public sector building programme, in the boom of the 1990s new housing came to mean simply private sector housing. Less obviously, but more importantly for our concerns, it has meant that, for better or worse, the public sector has abandoned one way in which it shaped the layout of the city. Today the role of the state has been reduced to the provision of major roads and the 'servicing' (local roads, sewerage, water, etc.) of developments organised by the private sector.

In this context much of Dublin has become an American-style 'edge city'. The commuter belt has spread as far as Dundalk, 90 kilometres from the city centre. Unlike in the previous period, new suburban housing has been almost entirely built for owner-occupation by private developers. Crucially development has been piecemeal, dictated largely by the ability of developers to purchase land and ensure that it is adequately serviced by the local authority for houses to be built. Dublin has extensive housing stock in need of repair and upgrading, but the tax system favours the construction of new housing, even though this is clearly less environmentally sustainable than renovation. In the new outer suburban areas the car has become essential: these areas have higher levels of new car registrations, higher levels of car ownership, higher levels of car journeys than the city centre (Williams and Shiels, 2002). Unlike in the 1970s, commuting is no longer necessarily from suburb to city centre, but from suburb to suburb as employment has also become suburban.

Beginning in the late 1960s central Dublin de-industrialised, a process that was effectively completed by the end of the 1980s, despite the attempts at urban regeneration through small scale IDA centres in the inner city. Industrial and manufacturing jobs moved to new industrial estates in what were then the inner suburbs. At the same time traditional industrial-type employment was rationalised to almost nothing, as on the docks or in Guinness. At the height of the unemployment crisis in the early 1980s Dublin had suffered worse job losses than the rest of the country. Yet the turnaround in employment has been dramatic. One key component of the boom was a new wave of foreign direct investment. Many US firms in electronics and above all software set up subsidiaries in Ireland, and far more so than before, this investment was concentrated in Dublin (Breathnach, 2000). Almost without exception, these jobs are in the new industrial estates and office parks in the outer suburbs, and with the exception of Intel's new railway station at Leixlip, they are not on any public transport route.

Since the late 1980s service industry employment has also become suburbanised. Until then office employment had remained in the city centre, the only change being that the DART shifted the centre of new employment away from the south inner city (Charlemont Street) in the early 1980s (MacLaran, 1999). By 2001 well over a third of all office space was located in the suburbs in purpose built office parks and 'science parks'.

Even more so than the earlier shopping centres, the new wave of retail parks and shopping malls are also completely car-centred. These new buildings have a high ratio of car parking space to floor space and are built on the assumption that all employees will come to work by private car (MacLaran and Killen, 2002). Even if they can be reached by public transport, the entire layout makes clear that the normal customer arrives by car and carries away purchases in the car. While the suburban outlets cater for extensive mass markets, retail in the city centre is specialising in niche and luxury markets, competing not so much with the suburbs but with other European cities such as Paris.

Finally, public institutions such as third level colleges and hospitals have expanded in the outer suburbs. Tallaght hospital in particular has replaced the city centre hospitals; the creation of the Tallaght and Blanchardstown Institutes of Technology and the expansion of the National University of Ireland Maynooth mean that third level education is no longer confined to the city centre and inner suburbs. Although such institutions can be reached by public transport, these radial public transport routes are largely irrelevant, since most people who use these suburban institutions travel from *other* suburbs.

The failure of planning

By the turn of the century Dublin's development into an American-style edge city had become unstoppable. This has nothing to do with any plans made by any public authorities; it is a genuine free-enterprise disaster.

In fact, civic planning for Dublin as a whole has been a contradiction in terms for most of the 20th century. Early plans such as the 1914 Civics Institute plan or the 1925 Civic Survey had virtually no effect on the city's development. The 1939 Dublin Sketch Development Plan foresaw replacing the inner city population with a prosperous 'urban bourgeoisie' as in other European cities, but in subsequent decades, as we have seen, the middle class flight to the suburbs continued. Although the Myles Wright plan of 1965 was never formally adopted, it did in fact provide the basis for the new suburban state sector housing estates. Subsequently, however, 'strategic planning' has had little impact on Dublin's development.

The clearest sign of this is the saga of Liffey Valley shopping centre. When it opened, Liffey Valley was advertised as 'Where the M50 meets the N4', thus making clear its location within a car-based city. The M50 had been planned and justified as a *ring road*, i.e. to take traffic out of the city centre and enable long-distance traffic to bypass Dublin. However, long before the first phase of the M50 opened to traffic in March 1990, the developer Tom Gilmartin had identified Quarryvale (the location of the Liffey Valley centre) as Dublin's most strategic location for a regional-scale shopping centre because it was at the fulcrum of the motorway bypass and the main road leading west. Development plans for the area foresaw a town centre at Neilstown next to the Dublin-Cork railway line to service the new housing areas of Lucan and Clondalkin, but once Quarryvale / Liffey Valley went ahead, any such development was undermined (McDonald, 2000: 213-218).

Given its location and size, it is estimated that the catchment area for Liffey Valley is a radius of 50 miles and 1.45 million potential customers. By the time Liffey Valley came to be built, the disadvantages of such mega shopping centres and in particular superstores were well established. Opponents of the centre included in particular RGDATA (the organisation of small retailers) and, ironically, the SIMI (because it feared the impact of cut-price petrol sales on its members' businesses). They were able to draw attention to studies abroad, especially in the UK, which documented the negative impact of out of town shopping centres on the urban fabric. Since then the UK evidence has mounted: between 1975 and 1990 the length of shopping journeys increased by 60%; one fifth of all local economic outlets closed between 1995 and 2000 (Simms et al, 2002). In Dublin the issue now is not so much the threat to large-scale retail in the city centre itself but the steady decline of more localised economies, especially in the inner suburbs. The local corner shop is usually more expensive than the supermarket, but taking it away creates a 'food desert' for those without cars. And for everyone in the vicinity, the local shop makes a crucial contribution to local life. It provides a space for casual social encounters, it ensures there are more 'eyes on the street' to watch over the neighbourhood (see Chapter 6).

Many details of the precise origins of the Liffey Valley project are now lost in lawyers' arguments in the Mahon Tribunal enquiry into planning corruption in Dublin. Yet the debate over corruption does not really explain how a development went ahead which completely undermined any chance of sustainable development in the west of Dublin. Part of the explanation is the extent of competition between local authorities in the area. The four Dublin local authorities are desperate for business that will improve their income from rates; they often therefore compete with each other to attract such large-scale developments. Thus the Liffey Valley shopping centre broke every rule of planning since it weakened the shopping centres already built or planned in Tallaght and Blanchardstown, but in order to enhance its rates basis, South Dublin County Council re-zoned the land for retail in 1993. Furthermore, the fact that local authorities have so few resources and effective strategic powers means that they are always likely to attract politicians whose vision of politics is limited to doing favours for their friends (or even finding friends for whom they can do favours). I return to this crucial issue of *governance* in Chapter 8.

Yet Quarryvale/Liffey Valley does depend utterly on public investment: without the M50 motorway it would not exist. The construction of the M50 has led to a scramble for land along its route between large-scale property consortia. Indeed, the entire expansion of shopping malls and retail parks in the west of the city is unthinkable without the M50, just as the new improved links to the airport, officially built to relieve congestion in the north of the city, are already leading to new out of town shopping centres. Road building in the greater Dublin area has thus become a mechanism for facilitating large scale property development, usually in ways that subvert the original justification for the roads. The boom of the last decade has accentuated the trend towards development being the result, not of any overall plan, but the accidental outcome of individual business decisions. Instead of creating a context in which developers' profits coincide with the overall public good, planning in the greater Dublin area has become at best a post hoc rationalisation. Just as in the USA, the profit strategies of private property interests are now linked to the city's suburbanisation. This is all the more difficult to change because of the growing importance of property and construction interests in the Irish economy. Unlike in the 1960s, major sections of the Irish business world are involved in private land holding, and it seems that, compared with some other European countries, these interests are particularly important in Ireland now. In other words, the particular pattern of development in Dublin has created opportunities for new interest groups that in turn have become entrenched and will be difficult to dislodge.

The trend towards the suburbanisation of Dublin as a car city can be traced back to the 1930s. However, it is really only in the last decade that these trends have accelerated to create a definitive break with the older transit city. The new sprawl is novel above all because it is entirely shaped by the motorcar. In the new suburbs of the edge city, reaching your home, doing your shopping, going out to meet friends or for entertainment, going to school, college or work – all really require you to use a private car. Certainly low-density is part of the problem, but as the example of Helsinki shows (Chapter 1), what is really decisive is that the development has been piecemeal and disconnected from any public transport provision that could concentrate activities around transport 'nodes'.

Growing suburbanisation has meant changes in the overall population of the greater Dublin area. As Figure 2.1 shows, as late as 1971 the population of Dublin City was greater than that of Dublin County and of the three counties of Kildare, Meath and Wicklow combined. By 1991

Dublin County (now divided into the three separate counties of Dun Laoghaire-Rathdown, Fingal, and South Dublin) had overtaken Dublin City. As in particular Frank McDonald and James Nix (2005) have documented, there has been even faster growth in what is now the outer suburban ring of Meath and Kildare as small local towns suddenly become transformed into dormitories of Dublin. Indeed, as Figure 2.1 again shows, by 2002 the population of these three outer counties by themselves was approaching that of Dublin City. At the same time, while the population between the canals is now growing for the first time since 1926, the population in some of the older suburbs of the city is actually declining.

Figure 2.1 Population Growth in the Greater Dublin Area: 1961-2002

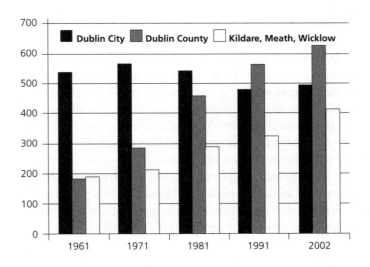

Source: *CSO, Census of Population 2002*

The astonishing growth of the Dublin metropolitan area in terms of population and wealth in the last decade has led to it being characterised as an emerging global city. Contemporary planning theorists often talk about such cities as 'polycentric mega-cities'. Indeed, this usage has been taken up by the most recent planning documents. In this model new development is focused on a limited number of nodes within the overall metropolitan space. These concentrations of population and economic activity justify extensive public transport connections. Since people move from one centre to another, rather than from the suburbs to the one central area, public transport is also facilitated: trains and buses do not all have to travel in the same direction at each peak journey, only to return empty in the opposite direction.

Increasingly, 'Dublin' is coming to mean the 'Greater Dublin Area', comprising the four Dublin councils plus Kildare, Meath and Wicklow. In population terms this is actually hardly a 'mega-city', for in European terms its population of 1.4 million is still relatively small. However, the metropolitan area is certainly now too big to be seen as simply an extension of the city centre. Some nodes of economic activity are clearly developing: Cherrywood, Sandyford, City West. Yet these concentrations are occurring not because they are close to public transport, but because they are close to major roads, above all the M50 ring road. Outside the city centre, Dublin is becoming what Americans term an 'edge city' – a largely unplanned growth along orbital motorways (Garreau, 1991).

In this situation, plans for polycentric development remain largely just another set of aspirations. Firstly, the key high prestige jobs are still concentrated in the city centre, especially in the International Financial Services Centre (IFSC) in the Docklands; there is little evidence that such jobs are dispersing into other centres in the suburbs (van Egeraat et al, 2006). Secondly, and far more importantly, all the offices and all the retail outlets at these nodes have been located on the assumption that employees and customers would arrive by private car: they are therefore a further incentive to car ownership. Within the last few years there have been a few attempts to move away from this model, above all the construction of what is effectively a new town at Adamstown. Adamstown is being built to make use of the nearby Dublin-Cork railway line and at a higher density so that moving around the area does not need a car either. Such developments show that private developers can be steered towards a much more sustainable development. However, Adamstown remains realistically just an oasis in a desert of sprawl. Indeed, without a massive upgrade of public transport it could even prove to be a major failure – on current trends trains that arrive in the new station will already be jammed with commuters travelling into Dublin from even further out.

The sprawl is interwoven with other social changes. Firstly and most obviously, it ensures that the average inhabitant of edge city spends more time moving around and travels further for the same tasks, than the average Dubliner of twenty years ago. Shopping, meeting friends or relatives, entertainment, all now require travelling greater distances than before, and these journeys probably take longer. The new Dublin is 'mobility intensive'.

Secondly, these journeys are now less concentrated at particular times of the day or the week. The most obvious example is work: the number of people working variable hours has been rising, as has the number of people working part-time. Going to work is not just a question of leaving home in the morning and coming home in the early evening, at the same time every Monday to Friday. In the new suburbs women are also particularly likely to be in employment, partly because the very high cost of housing means that it now requires two incomes to begin to purchase a family home. Because women are more likely to work part-time, this further adds to the overall variety of working times.

To some extent, the same variability applies to other

activities. For example, Ireland now has the longest shopping hours in the European Union, and people expect to be able to shop at any time of the day or week. One obvious consequence has therefore been the growth of Sunday shopping, particularly at the out-of-town shopping centres.

Finally, whereas twenty years ago most journeys were either very local, within the immediate vicinity, or from suburb to city centre, now journeys are to destinations which are less concentrated in particular areas. In edge city most journeys are from suburb to suburb and take on an almost random quality across the suburban space.

Increased physical movement, more variable journey times, and greater variety of destination – all of these are partly independent of suburban sprawl. They can also have different implications for public transport use in the city centre and in the suburbs. If – and this is a big if – the city centre has a good public transport system, then they actually increase public transport use, since more of the infrastructure is used for greater periods of time. For example, in central London the Underground is now as busy at weekends as in the week, thanks to varied working hours, leisure travel and weekend shopping. However, when these changes occur in the context of suburban sprawl, they accentuate the difficulties that unstructured and low-density developments create for public transport. Transit in transit city was well suited to moving large numbers of people at particular predictable times along radical routes from suburb to city centre. To the extent that movement in edge city is not like this, it is even more difficult to move people away from using their cars. Edge city is car city.

THE QUARANTINED URBAN RENAISSANCE

At the same time as edge city has emerged, so too has its apparent opposite, a new inner city Dublin. For more than ten years now, the population of Dublin between the canals has been growing again and new apartments between the canals even suggest the arrival of at least a distant cousin of 'prosperous urban bourgeoisie' with which the 1940 planners hoped to populate the inner city. Parts of the city centre have been regenerated, new public spaces created, and even before the arrival of Luas car traffic in the inner city started to be controlled.

Part of the revival of the centre of Dublin stems from some crucial decisions of central government. Unlike previous recessions, the crisis of the 1980s affected Dublin particularly badly. Clearly influenced by the apparent success of British government using private enterprise to regenerate London Docklands, the government set up a series of initiatives to attract private enterprise into the city.

One rather conventional policy was the use of tax incentives to encourage new housing in the city centre. Already by 1997 some 8,700 new dwellings had been built between the canals (MacLaran, 1999: 29). At one level this stimulation of the construction industry was a normal response of the Irish government to economic crisis. However, in two ways it was a clear policy shift. Firstly, it encouraged apartment buildings rather than the conventional suburban housing that Irish builders were used to churning out. Secondly, it also expanded the private rental sector by making it attractive to build apartments that the owners could buy in order to let. Landlords were no longer only the owners of decaying bed-sits in Rathmines. Conveniently this synchronised with and facilitated demographic and lifestyle changes. For the growing number of young single adults in professional type jobs, the housing market at last offered something other than the semi-detached suburban family house. The more affluent also began to solve their children's accommodation problem at university by buying an apartment. While the first apartments soon became notorious for their cramped space, the quality on the market has undoubtedly improved.

More fundamentally, and here the influence of London Docklands is clearest, regeneration of the city was kick-started by the central government creating new agencies outside the control of local government. Thus docklands was organised by the Customs House Docklands Development Board, later re-organised into the Docklands Development Board, which was responsible for the International Financial Services Centre (IFSC). This was the traditional policy of basing Irish economic development on foreign investment, but adopted for the contemporary service sector economy. Much to the chagrin of Ireland's EU partners, the policy has been successful, attracting mobile financial services to Dublin instead of to Continental Europe, even while those same countries have dutifully transferred money to Ireland through the EU structural funds. The real novelty of the IFSC was that selling Dublin was now not just about low tax or even about willing, obedient and appropriately educated employees, but about an attractive urban physical environment. The quality of Dublin as a city mattered in a way that it had never when foreign investment meant more semi-skilled assembly line jobs somewhere in the west of Ireland.

If the quality of the urban environment was a subordinate theme in the original IFSC project, it was central to Temple Bar, perhaps one of the most imaginative urban regeneration projects of its time in Europe and certainly in Ireland. Again the key mechanisms were tax incentives and a development organisation (Temple Bar Properties) outside of the existing administrative structures of Dublin City Council. Despite Temple Bar's subsequent emergence as the stag-party capital of Europe, the creation of an artistic and bohemian quarter in the middle of Dublin required real imagination. And for his role here, the now disgraced Taoiseach Charles Haughey does deserve some credit.

The IFSC and Temple Bar brought much needed new

ideas and new dynamism into the city. For all the criticisms of individual aspects of the projects, they created alliances between private enterprise and public authorities that generated employment and a new urban environment. Indeed, in both cases the urbanism was not an additional extra but fundamental to the success of the project. Subsequently, and only subsequently, Dublin City Council itself has been making its own contribution: the integrated area planning of Smithfield, the slow renovation of O'Connell Street, and the commitment to signature buildings and monuments in the city centre (the Millennium Bridge, the Spire, the Boardwalk along the river). The city centre has been enhanced by some restrictions on the private car: some limited pedestrianisation and above all the rigorous enforcement of parking controls. This has been a successful case of privatisation – subcontracting parking control to a private company has ensured that controls are enforced and are not subject to the various forms of favouritism and rule-bending that made parking restrictions a joke in the past. Dubliners now obey parking restrictions, for the simple reason they know they are likely to be penalised if they do not, and few would deny that the result has been an improvement. Controlling the car makes the city centre attractive, and at the same time has allowed greater numbers of people to reach it and to use it.

Merely limiting cars within the city centre, however, is a classic case of all sticks and no carrots. Without a public transport system, the car remains the only realistic way for most Dubliners to reach the city centre, thus creating pressure for car parking spaces that risk destroying the centre itself. Furthermore, the city centre remains a small area, its size limited by the distance that people can travel within it on foot.

Potentially the new Luas lines challenge this. Both lines do not merely replace existing car commuting journeys, but create new journeys bringing people into the city centre for recreation and shopping. Thus within the first few weeks of the Sandyford line opening, Grafton Street retail businesses were reporting fully 25% increase in turnover (Irish Times, August 2004). Rather less obviously, the Luas lines could enlarge the city centre itself, recreating Dublin as a 'pavement city'. Instead of simply using Luas to reach the city, Dubliners could use it to move around the city, riding a tram for example from Grafton Street to Mary Street...but that is not to be, because notoriously the two lines do not (yet) connect. As the next chapter shows, the fiasco of the disconnected Luas lines is symptomatic of Dublin's continuing wider traffic crisis – and of the disconnection between the pedestrianised city centre and the car-based edge city.

Chapter 3

What's wrong with Dublin transport?

When you arrive in most European cities, the tourist information office will give you a free visitor's map of the city, showing the city centre and how you can travel around using the public transport system. No such map is available in Dublin because of course the city does not have a public transport *system*. This chapter spells out what this means for the people who actually live in Dublin. After charting the extent to which public transport has declined despite recent improvements in the system, it examines the service's cost-effectiveness, its coverage of the city as a whole, the extent of innovation and the level of system integration. As we shall see, public transport in Dublin is actually quite cheap, but it is neither integrated nor innovative. As a result, Dublin is becoming not just a city in which people use cars but a city that is becoming *car dependent*.

THE CONTINUING DECLINE OF PUBLIC TRANSPORT?

The Dublin Transport Office's plan *Platform for Change* (DTO, 2000) remains the only overall plan for Dublin transport. The plan foresaw a massive shift from private car to public transport. Whereas in 1997 73% of all morning peak hour journeys to work in Dublin were by car, the plan set a target of 37% by 2016. On current trends there is no way that this target will be achieved.

In Ireland as a whole, people increasingly travel to work by driving their own car (59% of all journeys in 2002, up from 45% in 1981). Figure 3.1 shows this national picture: the rapid rise in the share of private car, especially during the 1990s, with a parallel decline in the share of journeys by bus, on foot and by bicycle. For other journeys the change is even more dramatic. For example, Figure 3.2 shows that in 1981 nearly a half of all children aged five to twelve walked to school and only a fifth were driven to school; twenty years later in 2002 the proportions were almost exactly reversed (although the distance travelled to school has increased in the period, the change is not big enough to account for this shift).

Figure 3.1 Travel to Work, Ireland 1981-2002

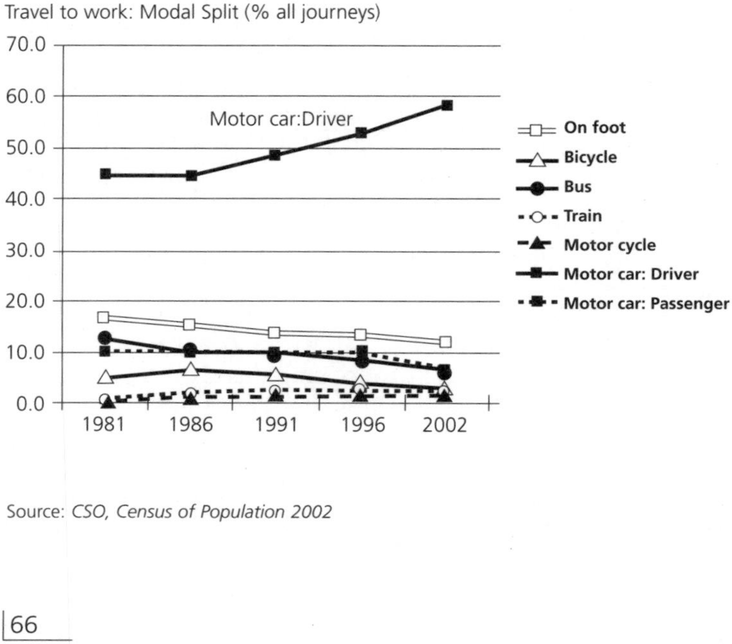

Travel to work: Modal Split (% all journeys)

Source: *CSO, Census of Population 2002*

Figure 3.2 Travel to School, Ireland 1981-2002

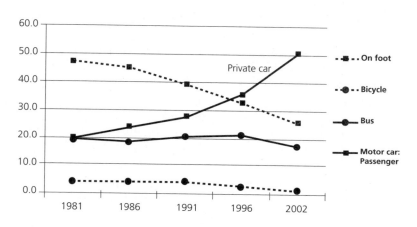

Source: *CSO, Census of Population 2002*

Compared with the country as a whole, the car is less important for these journeys within the Greater Dublin Area. For the journey to work the share of public transport is higher and the share of the private car is lower. In 2002 18% of all journeys to work were by bus and 47% by car. As Figure 3.2 shows, between 1996 and 2003 the share of the car rose and that of public transport fell. With continued economic growth concentrated in the Dublin area, it is hardly surprising that the absolute number of journeys to work has increased, and this has meant that the absolute number of people using the bus within the GDA has been increasing (1996 index=100; 2002 index=104.3). Nonetheless, the simple point remains: on this measure the car has become even more important as the means to travel to work, despite the declared policy objective of reducing this.

Certainly on some measures the situation does seem to be improving. The DTO 'headline' statistics focus on journeys to work that end within the GDA. This generates the much higher figure of 73% of journeys to work by car quoted in *Platform for Change*, but on this same measure there was an actual fall in the car share to 70% between 1997 and 2002. The DTO also reports a significant increase in the bus share of the modal split. The actual numbers of bus passengers in the morning peak rose by about 40% in the period 1997-2002 to a total of 85,000 (DTO, 2003)[1]. Over the last four years there have been further improvements in public transport provision – more Quality Bus Corridors (QBCs), Luas running at last, and significant extensions of the DART service. With deregulation taxis are much more widely available, and a few private bus companies have been allowed to open new routes. However, the results so far have been patchy: bus passenger numbers actually fell between 2003 and 2004 across the canal cordon, as did the numbers of cyclists and pedestrians (DTO, 2005).

Figure 3.3 Modal Split for Travel to Work, Greater Dublin Area Residents, 1996-2002

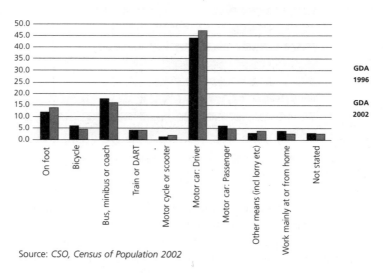

Source: *CSO, Census of Population 2002*

For many people what matters about the journey to work is simply how long it takes. Most journeys to work are now undoubtedly taking longer. And these journeys are not just by car, for long distance commuter train journeys are also increasing. Again, however, the picture is not all black. Set against the rise in long-distance commuting there is also a rise in shorter journeys to work. As Figure 3.3 shows, within the GDA there has been a decline in cycling but a larger rise in the proportion of people simply walking to work. This is clearly linked to the revival of the city centre (Chapter 2) so that the divided city also generates very different travel to work experiences.

Figure 3.4 Travel to Work or College, 12 Areas in Four Cities

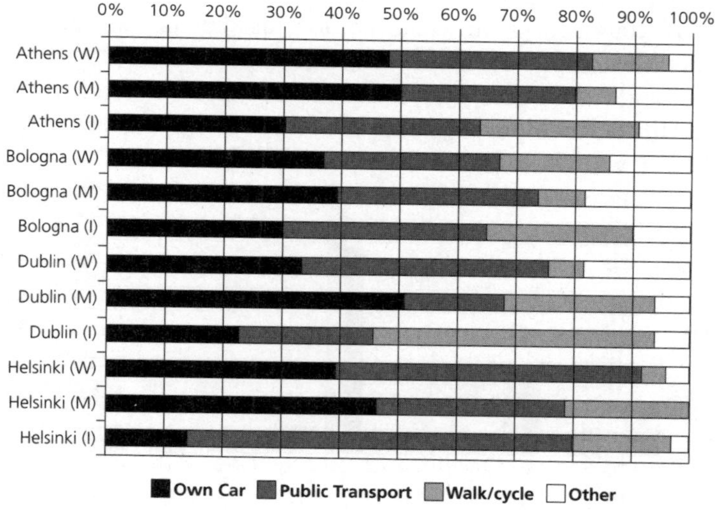

Source: *SceneSusTech survey*. Base: *all at work or college, N=456.*

Chapter 1 has already shown that by the 1990s car usage for the journey to work in Dublin was already higher than in most European cities. The SceneSusTech data shows how this operates at the local level: Dublin areas tend to have higher car usage and lower levels of public transport than broadly comparable areas in other cities. Thus Figure 3.4 shows the modal split for the journey to work or college for the twelve areas of all four cities in the study[2]: in middle class Dublin 51% travel to work by private car (the highest share in the entire study), and only 17% use public transport (the lowest in the entire study).

Much discussion of transport policy focuses on this modal split in the standard morning rush hour. However, this journey is a diminishing part of the total movements people make. Firstly, work itself is becoming more complex, with more people working non-standard hours (e.g. part-time or weekends), while increasing numbers report that they work 'variable' hours (Wickham, 2000). All the pointers are therefore that work is spread more through the day (and the night) than used to be the case – with important implications for the sort of transport people need to get to and from work. Secondly, the journey to work (whenever it occurs) does seem to be increasingly only one of the several journeys people make regularly. Here the car is particularly important – especially in Dublin.

There are no national or Dublin level figures for non-work journeys, but again the SceneSusTech material is useful. The study asked how people carried out a range of activities, such as shopping, visiting the doctor, socialising with friends, etc. Nearly three quarters of our respondents in Clonskeagh used the car to 'shop for food for several days' – by far the highest in the study. Equally, asked how they would reach a doctor for general medical care, people in middle class Dublin and middle class Athens were far more likely to use a car than people anywhere else, including comparable middle class areas of Helsinki and Bologna.

VALUE FOR MONEY ('ECONOMIC EFFICIENCY') AND SERVICE QUALITY

The usual way of evaluating public transport is in terms of 'efficiency' in terms of cost and value for money. Even if the service is subsidised or free to users, it is important that it is provided as cheaply as possible. Worthy claims on public resources are potentially limitless, and, everything else being equal, citizens and enterprises would rather pay as little tax as possible. Consequently, value for money is a crucial issue, even if as we shall see, it is hardly the only one.

As other studies have shown, Dublin Bus receives a relatively low subsidy (in terms of the ratio of subsidy to fare income) in comparison to public transport in many other European cities. There is less data available on Dublin's suburban rail services, but they do not seem to be particularly cost-effective in comparison to services elsewhere. Economic efficiency cannot, however, be discussed in terms of the immediate level of prices and subsidies for running costs. Quite apart from innovation (see below), investment in public transport systems has to be continually renewed. If this is not done, short-term performance and safety will suffer, and running costs may escalate.

Another aspect of efficiency is service quality. For public transport the quality of the service is what the public subsidy is 'buying'. The better the service, the better value the state is receiving. The perceived quality of public transport is also important for public policy, especially if the policy objective is to increase the share of journeys carried out by public transport. If the quality of public transport is perceived to be poor, then people will abandon it for the private car as soon as they possibly can, and public transport will remain a poor person's option. In general, affluent cities that have high levels of public transport usage also have transport systems that are viewed positively by inhabitants. Figure 3.5 compares perceptions of public transport quality in Athens, Bologna, Dublin and Helsinki from all of the 12 areas in the SceneSusTech study. It shows how the two cities with high private car usage, Athens and Dublin, are also the cities where public transport is held in low regard[3].

Figure 3.5 Perceptions of Public Transport Quality:
12 European City Areas 1999

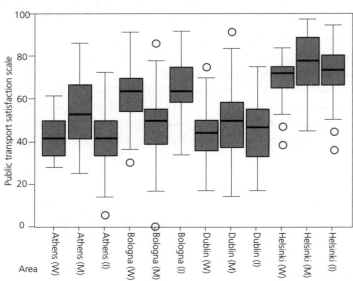

Source: *SceneSusTech survey*. Base: *all respondents, N=745.*

In fact, more detailed analysis (not shown here) shows that the problem in Dublin is even worse. In the other cities public transport users have a more positive perception of public transport than non-users (this finding is also reported by other research). This suggests that if non-users did shift to public transport, they would find public transport to be better than they expected. Consequently, policies that promote public transport are quite realistic. However, this is not the case in Dublin, where public transport users actually have a *lower* opinion of public transport than non-users. Indeed, according to our survey Dubliners who drive to work are more likely to enjoy the journey than those who use public transport, yet this difference is not nearly so clear cut and is sometimes reversed in the other cities. This of course suggests that public policy faces an additional obstacle in Dublin compared with other European cities.

In terms of service quality one crucial issue is the quality of information available to users. Public transport users need to know which routes go where and when a bus or train will arrive. In London the Underground map is part of the mental furniture of almost every inhabitant of the city, providing a map by which Londoners navigate themselves around the city. In Paris every bus stop has a clear map showing the route taken by each bus serving that stop, as well as the frequency of service; many stops now have electronic indicators showing in real time how long one has to wait until the next bus arrives. Stand at any bus stop in Dublin and you see the difference. If it has not been torn off, the bus timetable tells you really important information – the departure times of the bus from its terminus! When researchers interviewed people waiting at bus stops, most people only knew the bus route that they themselves used, but could not give any information about any other routes. Using the bus requires experience and a rather arcane knowledge, hardly a situation that encourages you to use the bus for a journey that you have never made before. The situation on the rail services is rather better. DART stations do have electronic indicators telling you the time of the next train, though they are notoriously unreliable. By contrast, Luas users find at every stop a clear chart of the line and a real time indicator that (nearly always) works. However, the point remains: there is no clear guide to public transport in Dublin as a whole.

A focus on cost efficiency also detracts from the crucial question of network *coverage*. How close is public transport to where people live and does it go where they want to go? In Dublin public transport is not particularly close to the public, even in the inner city and the older suburbs. Table 3.1 compares the three Dublin areas studied in the SceneSusTech project with their comparable areas in

Helsinki. It shows that in these areas the average time to the nearest public transport point in Dublin was around five minutes. By contrast, in the working class suburban area of Kontula it was only two minutes, in 'middle class' suburban Lansi Pakila four minutes, and in inner city Taka Töölö less than two minutes.

Table 3.1 Average Time to Nearest Public Transport Stop, Dublin and Helsinki

	Minutes
Jobstown	4.96
Clonskeagh	5.25
Docklands	4.98
Kontula	2.04
Lansi Pakila	3.55
Taka Toolo	1.52

Source: *SceneSusTech survey.*

The DTO's Platform for Change contains the target that 'in general' people should be within 10 minutes walking distance of a public transport stop (DTO, 2000: 7). In France one measure of 'social exclusion' used in official policy is living more than 10 minutes walk from public transport (Atkinson et al, 2002: 169). Although we do not have any clear figures on this for Dublin, it is likely that most people in Dublin's outer suburbs are socially excluded on this measure! Furthermore, even if transport links were improved in the suburbs, the problem is that most journeys to work are now suburb-to-suburb, rather than from the suburb to the city centre. A conventional bus route is of little use to many people working in the new office parks (McLaran and Killen, 2002).

In fact the situation is even worse than this. In most European cities the inner city area is well served by public transport, so coverage is only a problem in the expanding suburbs. In Dublin, however, many areas between the canals have no public transport in reach and there is little public transport that people can use for local journeys. Thus the SceneSusTech study included an inner city area of Helsinki (Taka Toolo) and North Docklands in Dublin. In the former over half of our survey respondents had used public transport in the last two days – including 43% with access to a car. In Docklands only 20% had used public transport, and these were all people without a car. Whereas planning policy in Dublin now aims for higher density in the city in order to reduce car usage, at the moment the policy is ineffective – because the necessary public transport does not exist. Effective public transport in the city centre would not simply be about bringing people into the city centre (in other words, strengthening the *transit city*) but would also allow people to move around within the city centre, in other words consolidating and expanding the *pavement* city.

INNOVATION

Another important measure of public transport success is the extent to which the system can innovate. How quickly and effectively can it respond to change? The most obvious issue is the response to new housing and employment patterns. For example, can new housing areas be serviced quickly? There are also changes in lifestyle that produce new transport needs, such as the development of late night clubbing in Dublin in the last few years. Yet transport enterprises should not simply react to change elsewhere, but also take the initiative themselves to improve. For this reason, it is useful to divide innovation into *process* and *product* innovation.

Process innovation in transport is the improvement of the existing 'product'. For example, ensuring that the staff is polite and helpful to customers, improving information systems (e.g. real-time timetables), better on board services on trains, changing schedules to adjust to new demands, etc. In Dublin the pace of change remains slow. Dublin Bus is only now piloting Real Time Passenger Information, and simpler (and cheaper) innovations, such as improved information (comprehensible timetables, legible route maps, on-bus destination indicators), are only occurring slowly. Despite public relations rhetoric, standards of customer service are low compared with some Continental operators. Although public subsidies for both Dublin Bus and Irish Rail are now linked to a 'Memorandum of Understanding' with the Department of Transport on service quality, it is not clear how this is meant to ensure that improvements actually happen.

Many process innovations can occur because front-line staff are willing and able to take initiative themselves. Thus the standard of information available when there are delays depends partly on the extent to which staff 'spontaneously' take the initiative, finding out what has gone wrong and telling passengers what they should do to reach their destinations. Since front-line staff know how the system functions (or does not function) and since they deal continually with passengers, they have valuable insights into how the service can be improved in ways that passengers will appreciate. Dublin Bus and Irish Rail provide obvious examples of the lack of such innovation. Dublin Bus's arcane timetables and incomprehensible signage has now become an international joke, while foreign visitors comment with incredulity on the apparent inability of DART staff to provide the simplest information about the service. Both organisations officially have 'partnership' structures for employee participation, but they have not made any contribution to such aspects of process innovation.

Product innovation involves the creation of new services and even new forms of service. Examples here range from new bus routes through to entire new rail systems.

Product innovation is not necessarily expensive, but it requires imagination and the ability to do things differently. The 'Aircoach' service from to Dublin city centre to Dublin airport provided by a private company and the Night Link services of Dublin Bus are examples of successful product innovation within the Dublin bus market. Significantly the first came from the private sector and the second partly from political pressure.

Successful product innovations obviously require a workforce able to work in new ways. They also require a range of management skills from marketing through to construction design and project management; they usually involve raising capital and, in public transport, political lobbying and coalition building. Large-scale product innovation requires large-scale contracts. The choice between 'make' or 'buy' is not simple, since even purchasing knowledge and equipment requires in-house competence to ensure that purchases are appropriate and cost-effective.

Process innovation usually involves using existing resources (equipment and staff) more effectively, but the same can apply to product innovation. Thus urban transport in many European cities has frequently been improved by developing new suburban services on unused or under-used railway lines; even in the UK in the last decade of its existence British Rail *opened* 200 railway stations (Wolmar, 2001).

When it was assumed that public transport was inevitably declining, then such innovation was not an issue at all. Good management meant the effective *management of decline*: keeping costs down, cannibalising parts of the service to keep more important services functioning etc. Where there is no rolling renewal programme, renewal will occur in response to short-term crises, usually about safety. The resulting investment will be inefficient, not least because the skills to manage such a programme are lacking, thus again 'proving' the inefficiency of the organisation. In the UK this was the situation of British Rail and London

Underground from the 1950s at least until the 1970s; it still applies to much of the UK urban bus industry.

In this situation of managed decline, cost containment is the overriding concern. If the system is losing money, increasing usage may simply mean losing more money and thus further strengthen the case for closing it down. Thus between 1987 and 1989 passenger usage on the DART system fell, thus *improving* financial results (Barrett, 1991). And if it is assumed that there is no political will to maintain the service, more passengers just mean more work for employees and more costs for managers. There is no incentive for staff to improve the existing service, and certainly no incentive for anyone to think of ways of expanding the service. The management skills needed to manage such a situation are real enough, but change and expansion require very different skills. If a transport system or transport provider is locked into decline, managers are unlikely to develop the skills to innovate. Managers will lack the skills to market existing services, lack the ability to 'see' new market openings; organisational change becomes simply a threat and a codeword for further deterioration in quality of service.

Today Dublin Bus and Irish Rail have partially emerged from such a situation. Almost unnoticed, Irish Rail has been able to develop new infrastructural projects such as the DART upgrade – and complete them on time and in budget. Clearly, however, change and innovation are not yet on the scale needed to ensure that change in public transport at least keeps pace with the changing city. Major change requires major investment, but also renewed organisations.

NETWORK INTEGRATION

Transport provision in a city should be evaluated in terms of the extent to which it provides an integrated network or system rather than simply a series of discrete routes. Such integration can be within modes (changing from one bus to another) or between modes (e.g. from bus to rail). Network integration is not just a question of convenience, it expands the extent to which people will routinely use public transport and it increases the range of destinations and the types of journeys. In a well-integrated system, passengers can move from one part of the city to another, rather than being restricted to particular transport routes. By the 1920s, the major European cities had such transport systems. The metro in Paris is a classic example of a well-integrated single mode transport system. And the Parisian metro is integrated with the high-speed suburban rail system (the RER) and now the new tramways, as well as with bus routes.

A well-integrated, multi-modal system requires connecting routes and interchange stations, and so requires investment. However, much integration can be achieved at relatively low cost by better co-ordination of existing facilities. Indeed, major improvements can often be achieved simply by better route maps and inter-operable ticketing. One way to gauge whether or not a city has an integrated system is simply the extent to which there are maps of the system on display.

Where there is an integrated transport system, the route map will resemble a grid rather than the spokes of a wheel: the system allows people to move around the city for many different reasons. An integrated transport system allows people to live and work in the city, but also to socialise, to shop, to go to the cinema, etc. An integrated system therefore is not just about moving people from the suburbs to the city centre and back again, a form of mobility which as we have seen is of decreasing relative importance, given that most employment as well as most housing is now in the suburbs.

The suburbanisation of cities poses challenges for network integration. A transport grid is obviously easier to create in a high-density central city area (for example, in Dublin between the canals) than across the metropolitan area of a large contemporary city. Network integration thus raises questions of land use planning. This is often posed as a question of population density, but this is to over-simplify. As Chapter 1 has already shown, Athens, a high population density city, has poor public transport, while Helsinki, a city with as low a population density as Dublin, has a very effective public transport system and low levels of car usage. In Helsinki, land use planning and transport planning are integrated, so that new developments, whether for housing, shopping or employment, are concentrated at transport nodes.

In terms of network integration Dublin clearly scores very badly. Public transport in Dublin is a classic example of an almost totally unintegrated system (indeed the word 'system' hardly applies to the provision of public transport in Dublin). It is unfortunately only too typical of Dublin that a previous Minister for Public Enterprise, Mary O'Rourke, in all seriousness decided that the Luas, up to then the most expensive investment in public transport in the city for twenty years, should comprise two lines that did not even connect with each other. What is striking is that this *lack* of integration has occurred, even though all the public transport in the city is ultimately supplied by the same company. Here CIÉ has been a complete failure. Although buses and trains are state-owned, they have not been integrated into a system even in terms of integrated route maps, co-ordinated timetables and integrated ticketing. This failure is a shameful squandering of public assets by several generations of senior management and the politicians to whom they ultimately answered.

PUBLIC TRANSPORT AND CAR DEPENDENCY

In Dublin car ownership is widespread, even though not every household, let alone every adult, actually owns a car.

The car is used not just for the journey to work, but for the increasing number of other journeys people make. However, such extensive car ownership or even car usage does not in itself prove car dependency. When it is claimed that Belfast is the UK's 'most car dependent city' (Cooper et al, 2001), this is strictly speaking unproven, since it is merely deduced from the fact that car *usage* is higher in Belfast than elsewhere. Car dependency, Chapter 1 argued, means that ordinary daily activities require journeys that can only be made by car.

In these terms many areas of Dublin are not strictly speaking car dependent, at least as far as the journey to work is concerned. Thus in the SceneSusTech survey in the middle class Dublin area of Clonskeagh only 14% of all journeys to work were car dependent in the sense that car drivers claimed that they had no 'reasonable' alternative. Although they habitually used their car to get to work, they were aware of other possibilities, above all public transport. Indeed, in such areas improvements in the quality of existing public transport services can persuade some people to abandon their cars. Shortly after we completed our survey, the first QBC was introduced and this change did lead to a substantial increase in bus usage in the area.

In a suburb like Clonskeagh, the situation is very different for non-work journeys. Here not only do people overwhelmingly travel by car but they find it difficult to imagine any alternative mode of transport for these journeys. Interestingly, just as Clonskeagh does have some public transport, so our respondents also reported that they did have some facilities such as a shop or a pub within what they considered 'walking distance'. Nonetheless, most people used their cars for shopping, for visiting friends and for entertainment. Local facilities are increasingly being abandoned for ones further away: the car allows greater choice and so car ownership has led to new journeys which could not be made without a car.

These results suggest that for car owners the relationship between overall levels of car usage and car dependency may be *curvilinear*. Where few people use cars, car dependency for those who do use a car is high: people are using their cars to make new journeys for which a car is absolutely necessary (as Chapter 5 will show, this can also occur where public transport is so good that most people can and do use it to reach their workplace). As car usage rises, people use cars for journeys for which other forms of transport are still available but which now they seem inferior to the car. Finally, as car usage continues to rise, other modes of transport decay, and increasingly the city is built on the assumption that everyone does have a car: car usage becomes 'essential' and car dependency for car owners becomes complete.

Figure 3.6 shows the relationship between car dependency and car usage for non-work journeys in all the SceneSusTech case study areas[4]. It shows three clusters of areas: one of low car usage and medium car dependency (Helsinki Inner and Working, Dublin Inner and Working, Athens Inner); one of medium car usage and low car dependency (Bologna Middle and Working, Helsinki Middle); a final cluster of high car usage and high car dependency (Athens Working and Middle, Dublin Middle). In other words, for non-work journeys car dependency at first does fall as car usage rises: as more people use cars, they make journeys for which there remain alternative modes of transport. However, as car usage continues to increase, more and more journeys are made for which the car is the only possible form of transport.

Figure 3.6 also shows how the relationship varies by city. In Bologna and Helsinki, as car usage rises, so car dependency falls. By contrast, in Athens and Dublin, as car usage rises car dependency increases. This is consistent with the better quality public transport *system* in Bologna and Helsinki as compared with the other two cities: people are choosing to make journeys by car, but there are still public transport alternatives even for many non-work journeys. By contrast in Athens and Dublin, increasing car usage means that people are making more journeys (e.g. suburb-to-suburb) for which there are no public transport alternative.

Figure 3.6 Car Dependency and Car Usage in 12 Areas: Non-work Journeys

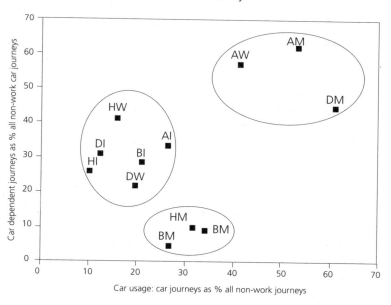

Source: *SceneSusTech survey.*

Key to Figure 3.6

AW	Athens – Working class	AM	Athens – Middle class	AI	Athens – Inner city
BW	Bologna – Working class	BM	Bologna – Middle class	BI	Bologna – Inner city
DW	Dublin – Working class	DM	Dublin – Middle class	DI	Dublin – Inner city
HW	Helsinki – Working class	HM	Helsinki – Middle class	HI	Helsinki – Inner city

CONCLUSION: EVALUATING PUBLIC TRANSPORT

This chapter has presented different criteria for evaluating public transport. It has shown that the apparently simple criterion of 'economic efficiency' is totally inadequate as a criterion for judging a public transport system. Public transport is – or at least can be – an integral part of a European city. As such, there are many different criteria by which a system can be judged.

Even by itself, 'economic efficiency' turns out to be more complicated than it appears because of the need to account for ongoing investment in the system and to measure service quality. Obviously there is a question of value for money, but this depends also on the purpose of spending the money in the first place. Subsequent chapters will argue that effective urban public transport is important for environmental sustainability, social inclusion and social cohesion. If public transport is to achieve this it has to be efficient and cost-effective, but these terms turn out to involve rather more than perhaps many advocates of 'competition' would accept.

Perhaps the best single measure of a successful public transport system is the extent to which people do *not* use the private motorcar. In these terms Dublin's transport system is a failure. In terms of a very narrow definition of economic efficiency, Dublin Bus (though presumably not Irish Rail) appears to score quite well. As Chapter 7 will show, franchising routes and/or privatising Dublin Bus will create new problems that are completely irrelevant to the overall issue of improving other – and more important – aspects of Dublin's transport system.

A rational debate about public transport in Dublin would focus on how to reduce car dependency, and any discussion of the 'economic efficiency' of public transport should be within this context. There is not much point in having an 'efficient' public transport system that is only

used by the very poor, with perhaps a few prestige projects
used by the more affluent.

Notes:

1   The DTO figures are different from those in the census for at
     least two main reasons. The census figures are based on respon-
     dents' place of *residence* within the GDA, while DTO figures
     refer to *journeys* within the GDA. Thus the census will omit
     long-distance commuting into the GDA from its figures on the
     GDA. The census also involves all journeys to work, whatever
     time they originate, while the DTO figures refer to journeys
     ending in the morning peak.

2   See Appendix for full list of local areas and their abbreviations.

3   In the chart the solid black line indicates the average (median)
     score for each group; the 'box' indicates the spread of the each
     quarter of values above and below the average; the thin lines or
     'whiskers' and the circles show the range of the other values.
     Thus people in all the Helsinki areas not only give higher scores
     to public transport, the scores are more concentrated (there is
     greater agreement) than in most other areas.

4   See Appendix for full list of local areas and their abbreviations in
     the chart.

Chapter 4

Fat and dirty Dublin?

C ar dependency leads to three different sets of problems: environmental damage, social exclusion and poor quality of urban life. This chapter examines the first of these. For most people, the main argument for reducing car usage is probably pollution. In some vague sense, people are aware that cars are 'bad for the environment'. Analysis of the environmental impact of cars shows that some environmental damage is more direct than others, although overall it is certainly true that everyone suffers in the long run from car usage and in the long run everyone will benefit from reducing it.

Chapter 1 has already shown that there is no automatic linkage between a city's wealth and the level of car usage. Dublin's car problem is not some automatic consequence of 'affluence', 'progress', 'globalisation' or any other excuse that politicians may wish to wheel out. Does a similar argument apply to cars' environmental impact? A key issue is the extent to which economic growth can be 'decoupled' or 'delinked' from environmental damage. Achieving such uncoupling may involve humanising the car by reducing its negative impact, but it may also involve social changes that reduce the demand for car travel altogether. As we shall now see, while some aspects of the car can be reformed, others are more intractable and demand more radical and over-arching social and political changes.

DIMENSIONS OF ENVIRONMENTAL DAMAGE

The car impacts on the natural environment in different ways, from local exhaust emissions to greenhouse gasses, energy use and land use. These are listed in the first column of Table 4.1, which also lists some impacts of the car on humans – noise, accidents and a physically unhealthy lifestyle.

The table is also useful for highlighting the different issues raised by these different impacts, for these 'car problems' have several different dimensions. The second column of the table sketches the *scale* at which they impinge on the environment. Thus local exhaust emissions damage the environment in the immediate vicinity of the car, whereas carbon dioxide emissions damage the global environment. At the intermediate level are issues such as land usage, which are above all a problem at the level of the city and of the nation. It is plausible that there will be more political will to tackle local scale problems, since the people who are affected by them are easily identifiable. By contrast, global scale problems affect the whole world, which means that it is always possible to hope that someone else will tackle them.

Table 4.1 Cars Problems: Scales and Time Horizons

Issue	Scale	Time	Sustainability threat	Current 'coupling'
Local emissions	Local / urban	Immediate risks	No	Relatively uncoupled
Greenhouse gasses	Global	Medium term	Yes	Coupled
Noise	Local / urban	Immediate	No	Relatively uncoupled
Land usage	Urban / national	Medium-long term	Possibly	Coupled
Energy usage	National	Short to medium term	Possibly	Coupled
Deaths	Local	Immediate	No	Relatively uncoupled
Health	Local	Short term	Possibly	Coupled

The third column of the table looks at the question of time involved. Some damage is experienced immediately, as in the case of deaths from car accidents, unpleasant noise or noxious fumes. Other forms of damage are more insidious, in that their effects will only really be experienced in the future. Once again this means that political pressure to tackle the issue will be weaker. This applies in particular to issues such as land usage, energy usage and – to some extent – greenhouse gasses.

As the fourth column of the table suggests, not all environmental damage caused by the car can really be considered to threaten environmental sustainability. Sustainability was initially defined as 'meeting the needs of the present without compromising the ability of future generations to meet their needs' (Haberl et al, 2004 citing WCED, 1987). More recent definitions include notions of equity and fairness between and within societies, but this seems to confuse social and environmental issues. There is in fact no logical reason why sustainable societies should always be more egalitarian than unsustainable ones, even though, as the next chapter will show, a car dependent society does tend to exacerbate social inequality.

The final column of the table indicates the relationship between these impacts and economic growth. Damage can be 'coupled', i.e. growing at the same pace as the economy; it can be 'relatively uncoupled', i.e. growing more slowly than the economy; or it can even be 'absolutely uncoupled', i.e. actually falling even though the economy is growing (Haberl et al, 2004). The most optimistic case is that of local emissions, which appear to have been largely uncoupled from economic growth, and although this may appear surprising, the same actually applies to deaths from car accidents. By contrast, greenhouse gasses remain firmly coupled to economic growth, although even here, as we shall see, some countries are more polluting than others at the same level of economic output.

LOCAL POLLUTION

Cars produce a cocktail of pollutants. They do so not just from their exhausts, though this is the main cause, but also through their braking systems and even simply through their tyres rotating on the road. Lead is harmful especially to pregnant women, carbon monoxide is potentially life threatening if it enters the bloodstream, benzene is carcinogenic, nitrogen dioxide and PM10 (minute dust particles also produced by cars) damage the lungs, while nitrogen dioxide also helps form acid rain.

Nonetheless, here most authorities consider there have been dramatic improvements. In Ireland these have occurred because EU regulations have imposed higher standards on car manufacturers and because EU regulations require common methods for monitoring and reporting pollution levels. Within Dublin, Dublin Bus from 2002 began to change over to low sulphur diesel fuel, which has dramatically cut particulate emissions (Dublin Bus, 2003).

Dublin City Council monitors levels of air pollution through a small network of monitoring stations. The methodology and the maximum permitted levels of pollutants are all the result of EU directives. According to the most recent reports, levels of lead in the atmosphere were well below permitted levels; levels of carbon monoxide (also partly produced from car exhausts) were falling and 'comfortably' below the level defined as dangerous to human health; benzene (contained in unleaded petrol) was also below the safety level. However, levels of nitrogen dioxide, also produced by cars, were only just below the safety threshold, and particulate PM10 were above the limits at some monitoring sites (Dublin City Council, 2003; DTO, 2005: 39).

Pollution levels are obviously higher where there are more streets with heavy traffic. Presumably this means that pollution levels are higher in the inner city. This raises an issue often ignored in environmental discussions: *who* is on the receiving end of environmental damage? Whereas twenty years ago this would have meant that middle class commuters were poisoning working class housing areas, changes in the city's social structure make this probably less the case today.

Overall then local pollution from the car in Dublin is certainly now *relatively* uncoupled from economic growth and some aspects are probably *absolutely* uncoupled. This success story would seem therefore to be an example of what economists now term an Environmental Kuznets Curve which measures the relationship between material affluence (measured by GDP per capita) and environmental impacts. This normally takes the form of an inverted U: as economies grow, the environmental impact rises with greater material consumption, but then falls as resources are devoted to pollution control (Friedl and Getzner, 2003). To the extent that this occurs, society can be seen as adapting technology in line with environmental requirements, a process that sociologists refer to as 'ecological modernisation' (Hajer, 1995).

GREENHOUSE GASSES

In global terms the main damage caused by cars is their contribution to global warming. Cars produce 'greenhouse gasses', above all carbon dioxide (CO_2). Solar energy radiating from the sun reaches the earth and then radiates back into space; greenhouse gasses trap some of this energy and so maintain the earth's temperature. Human activity has been increasing the amount of greenhouse gasses in the atmosphere, thus increasing the extent to which solar energy is retained and thus creating global warming.

Despite the attempts of the US government to downplay the issue, global warming now seems incontrovertible.

We are already seeing the results of human-induced climate change – melting snowcaps in the mountains, rising sea water levels, more extreme temperatures and storms. Within fifty years, according to a recent European Environment Agency report, three quarters of the glaciers in the Alps will have melted. Indeed, CO_2 levels are now at their highest for fifty-five million years, prompting the UK government's Chief Scientific Advisor, Sir David King, to declare that climate change is a bigger threat than global terrorism (Connor, 2004).

Not content with making the largest contribution to global warming of any nation, the USA refused to sign the 1997 Kyoto protocol that set targets to reduce greenhouse gas emissions. By contrast, the EU (pre-2004 enlargement states) agreed to reduce emissions by 8% over twenty years.[1] Amongst themselves the EU member states made a 'burden sharing' agreement, in which richer members agreed to disproportionately reduce their emissions, pre-cisely to ensure that the development of the poorer mem-bers was not held back by environmental controls. Thus Germany committed itself to reduce its emissions by 21%, but Ireland was allowed to *increase* its emissions by 13%. As of now Ireland will not even make this target. Despite the existence of a 'national climate strategy' (Department of the Environment, 2000), there is little evidence that any major political party has any serious plans to achieve the targets. Irish greenhouse gas emissions fell after 2001, but largely because of the once-off replacement of coal-fired with gas and oil-fired generating stations.

As both the European Environment Agency and the (Irish) Environment Protection Agency report, the key problem in Ireland as in most other countries is the contin-uing rise in emissions from transport. Here road transport is by far the main culprit, although the impact of air travel is now increasing rapidly. Thus agriculture remains the biggest contributor to Ireland's greenhouse gas emissions, but this has only increased by 3.2% between 1990 and 2003. By contrast, those from transport increased by an astounding 129.4%. Worse still, whereas energy and industry total outputs are now declining, that of transport continues to increase. This shows that while in Ireland some forms of environmental pollution are now at least *relatively* uncoupled from economic growth, car emissions are still coupled with economic growth (see Figure 4.1).

Figure 4.1 Growth, Green House Gasses and Energy Usage: Transport in Ireland 1990-2003

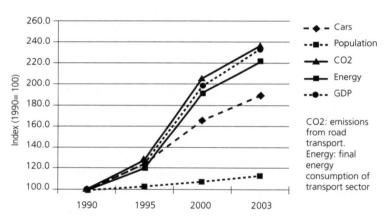

Source: *CSO, Environment – Principal Statistics; CSO, National Income & Expenditure, 2004.*

Measuring the actual output of carbon dioxide involves a series of assumptions and estimates. Essentially the level of carbon dioxide is assumed to depend on the quantity of fuel purchased, adjusted for factors such as the type of engines in use, driving speeds etc. The figures are further complicated by 'fuel tourism' – much fuel purchased in the Republic is actually used abroad and in Northern Ireland (EPA, 2004: 161). Yet even after taking account of such factors, it is clear that in Ireland greenhouse gas emissions from transport are rising roughly in line with economic growth.

Since carbon dioxide is produced as fuel is consumed, the simplest way to reduce cars' CO_2 emissions is to reduce the amount of petrol used. In theory CO_2 emissions could be reduced by technological change that makes car engines more fuel-efficient. If this were the case, then the normal 'Environmental Kuznets Curve' would apply to this aspect of car transport, but it does not seem to be happening. The problem is that while cars have been becoming more fuel efficient, they are also becoming heavier and more powerful. For example, in Ireland in 1990 cars with engines of over 1501cc made up 39% of new car registrations; by 2005 the figure was 51%. At the top of the range, cars of over 2401cc were 1% of new registrations in 1990, but 5% in 2005. The shift is epitomised by the dreaded SUVs and the apparently insatiable desire of some car owners to roam the streets of Dublin in cars marketed for their off-road looks: very nearly one third of all the new Land Rovers in Ireland in 2005 were registered in Dublin City and County! (CSO, 2006).

Globally emissions from transport amount to 25% of carbon dioxide emissions; road passenger transport (i.e. essentially cars) comprises about half of this. Everywhere emissions from cars are increasing and it is everywhere clear that uncoupling these emissions from economic growth will require radical policy changes (e.g. Olsthoorn, 2003). However, it is important to notice that although car transport emissions remain coupled to economic growth everywhere, different countries have different base lines. Thus the USA creates more greenhouse gasses per capita than other countries not just because the USA is rich, but also because Americans use cars extensively and furthermore car usage in the USA is particularly energy inefficient (with higher fuel consumption for every passenger kilometre) (Olsthoorn, 2003). This national variation suggests that reducing car usage is not only essential if transport green-house gasses are to be reduced, it is actually possible.

It is often claimed that technological fixes are available for CO_2 as for other emissions. This is debatable. Diesel produces less CO_2 than petrol, but more carcinogenic emissions. Bio-fuels (e.g. ethanol made from grain) do burn more cleanly than petrol, but it is not clear that there is enough land to produce the amount of grain needed. Much more realistic alternatives seem to be electric batteries or, most promising of all, hydrogen fuel cells. Since both depend on electricity to be generated, in one sense they simply move the problem from the car to the electricity generating station. However, their great advantage is that electricity can be generated in different ways, some of which are clean or at least do not produce as much carbon dioxide (nuclear, hydro, wind).

Certainly it is possible to imagine a change-over to less polluting forms of car, even though this requires not just solving the problems of engineering but major modifications of the car system as a whole – fuel stations and fuel suppliers, maintenance workshops, etc. However, the mounting evidence of accelerating climate change means that we need to restrain car usage now, rather than waiting for a silver bullet that may turn out to be made of lead.

There is a final – and scandalous – argument for doing nothing in Ireland. It could be claimed that Ireland's contribution to global warming is so small that Ireland should wait until the big nations change. In fact this is what the Irish government is doing. Yet global warming is now an urgent problem. Economic growth in India and China now means that the world car population is growing faster than the world's human population: the generalisation of American, or even European, levels of car-produced green-house gasses to the rest of the world will guarantee global disaster. Rich countries can only plausibly argue for a more sustainable form of growth if they themselves show that they can reduce their emissions – and the starting point is ratification of the Kyoto protocol. The Irish government's decision (10 September, 2004) to abandon plans for a carbon tax shows that it has in fact no intention of meeting its Kyoto targets, and sotto voce, would be happy if Kyoto was abandoned, not least since the treaty foresees fines for countries not meeting their agreed targets. Instead of standing up to the USA over Kyoto, Irish diplomats may well be going to be quietly trying to sabotage the European Union's commitment to Kyoto.

ENERGY AND MATERIAL USAGE

Worldwide, all forms of transport are now almost completely dependent on oil, and transport in turn uses about 60% of all oil products. Within the transport sector road users (passengers and goods) use about 80% of the oil, most of the rest going to air transport (OECD, 1996: 10). Cars (and lorries) are therefore responsible for somewhere around half of total oil consumption.

Claims that 'the oil is about to run out' have been made since the 1970s, and are notoriously unreliable. Shortages make further exploration worthwhile, and price rises make previously unprofitable wells viable. However, none of this detracts from the simple fact that oil is a non-renewable resource that is being depleted at an increasing rate. Furthermore, the developed world's reliance on oil creates dependence on unsavoury and unstable regimes, such as Saudi Arabia. One would expect that in this situation any vaguely rational government would be trying to reduce the country's consumption of oil. Remaining so dependent on oil means that the form of economic growth is both environmentally unsustainable and extremely vulnerable to short term instability.

Reducing oil consumption is therefore desirable on

economic, strategic and environmental grounds. In the short term price rises through a carbon tax will have some impact, since one effect is to penalise those who insist on driving powerful and/or heavy cars that consume much petrol. However, the problem here is that any tax increase will be unpopular, while the evidence is that only major price increases will have any impact. Thus the sudden petrol price increases after the first oil shock of 1973 did reduce the West's petrol consumption, forcing people to drive more economically and making energy efficient cars more popular. However, this effect did not last much longer than a decade. Today, more than thirty years later, in Ireland total petrol consumption by private cars is firmly coupled to GDP (see Figure 4.1).

Posing the issue in such terms ignores the structural problem. Car dependency means that whatever sort of car people drive, they drive because their overall lifestyle depends on having a car. This is what makes the demand for petrol relatively unresponsive to price changes. Ultimately people have to be enabled to choose whether to use a car or not, and this means reducing car dependency itself.

LAND USAGE

While the car's consumption of oil is well known, it is less appreciated how the car system in its entirety guzzles other resources. The most obvious is land.

Firstly, roads take up ever increasing space. During the heyday of interstate highway construction in the 1960s, it has been estimated that 50,000 people each year were displaced from their homes by roadway construction in the US (Freund and Martin, 1993:19). Today, according to one estimate in the USA, 'we pave an area equal to the state of Delaware every year' (Duany et al, 2001:12). Land used for roads is usually good agricultural land (because roads run along valleys). Look out of an airplane window while flying over western Europe: on a clear day at cruising height you can see the motorways, but not the railway lines.

Cars also take up space *within* cities. According to the OECD, various imprecise estimates have been made as to the actual proportions of urban land consumed by the car. The range most often cited is that 25-35% of the land is devoted to streets in modern cities, compared with less than 10% in cities designed before the advent of motorised transport. These proportions do not include land used for auxiliary transport purposes, such as parking. Within UK residential areas such as housing estates, at least one fifth is taken up by roads and parking (TEST, 1991:172). In new American suburban cities land used for roads can reach up to two thirds of the total space. However, there are clear differences between the USA and Europe. As the authors of *Suburban Nation* describe, many American cities have almost destroyed their city centres for the car; their newer suburbs sprawl across the countryside, designed on the assumption that everyone has a car and built with vast road networks (Duany et al, 2001). According to one estimate with data from 1980, the average American city has more than three times more road per person than the average European city (Newman and Kenworthy, 2003).

Out in Edge Dublin cars use up space, American style. Each new motorway exchange uses the amount of land of a village centre; the new office parks and supermarkets are surrounded by acres of parking. And above all, sprawl involves asphalt: needlessly wide roads within the estates and ample carports for every house (since every adult resident needs a car). If the roads to the estates often still remain country lanes, the pressure of cars will ensure that they are soon widened. Although the consumption of land by the car is something everyone can see, it is not yet officially even recognised as an environmental problem. In fact, however, the car's consumption of space seems to be one of

the most fundamental ways in which contemporary society, despite the decline of manufacturing industry, remains
resource-intensive (Fischer-Kowalski and Amann, 2001).

At the same time, the inner city is almost going in the
opposite direction. Bizarre though it may seem now, the
pedestrianisation of Grafton Street was initially controversial, but since then many more streets have been successfully pedestrianised and space reclaimed from the car.
Above all, the plans of the 1970s to drive urban ring roads
through the city (the Inner Tangent) have been abandoned,
so that at least for the moment road building between the
canals is at a standstill, with only the Eastern By Pass still a
shadow on the horizon. In fact it is in the older suburbs that
land is still being lost to the car: the big road schemes in particular, such as the completion of the M50, and the steady
replacement of gardens with parking lots.

All of this land loss is not just an aesthetic issue. Road
construction is itself a use of material resources. Paved
roads not only consume petroleum in the form of asphalt
but can also decrease the ground's capacity to retain rain-
fall, which can increase flooding. Extensive paving disrupts
the natural hydrologic cycle, particularly in its depletion of
groundwater supplies. The run-off of auto wastes into adja-
cent lands is enormous. For example, it has been calculated
that each year 100,000 tons of fine dust from tyre abrasion
is generated on the former West Germany's roads and 1mm
of surface is rubbed off the network of roads (Freund and
Martin, 1993: 27). An adverse environmental impact of such
paving is typically the increased flushing of pollutants into
watercourses, rather than their slow dispersal within natural drainage systems (OECD, 1996:20). And finally, paving
over more land, whether by motorways or even by drive-
ways, reduces bio-diversity.

NOISE

We live in increasingly noisy times and noise is bad for you. Repeated exposure can result in long-term hearing damage, stress and loss of sleep. Furthermore, our bodies do not, it seems, just adapt to higher levels of noise: continued high levels of noise remain stressful.

Noise is measured on a logarithmic scale, known in abbreviated form as the dB(A) scale. As noise varies in its intensity it is necessary to define the time over which the noise is measured; the noise readings are then averaged over that period. This is referred to as the Leq measurement. A daily Leq of greater than 65dB(A) is normally taken as an absolute limit and is used in regulations concerning sound insulation compensation (Whitelegg, 1993).

By 1990 it was estimated that 130 million (16%) of the population of OECD countries were exposed to noise levels over 65dB(A), in comparison with 100 million in the early 1970s (ECMT, 1990). Furthermore, more than 50% of the population of OECD countries were exposed to noise levels in excess of 55dB(A), and this proportion was increasing all the time (ECMT, 1990:23). According to the same research review, the noise that disturbs most people is road traffic, followed by neighbourhood and aircraft noise (ECMT, 1990:21/2).

Cars produce noise in many different ways: from the engine, the air inlets, the exhaust and cooling system, so-called rolling noise (from the car moving though the air and the cars' tyres moving on the road surface), brakes and rattling car bodies. To this list should now be added on-board sound systems. Certainly, there has been technological progress in limiting car noise (better tyres, better road surfaces, muffled exhausts, quieter transmission etc.) (Whitelegg, 1993:66). At the same time cars are now fitted with more and more powerful sound systems, enabling culturally challenged young men to drive around imposing their musical tastes on all and sundry. More generally, and as in so many other areas, technical improvements are cancelled out by the growth in the number of cars, the growth in the number of car journeys and in this case in particular, the growth in the number of HGVs. In residential areas, a more effective strategy lies in changing how drivers behave. 'Traffic calming' forces drivers to drive more slowly, and thus more quietly. Where traffic is heavy, one solution may appear to be double-glazing and acoustic engineering. However, this technical fix breaks the connection between the houses and the street, so in turn reducing sociability (and possibly even driving up car usage).

In Ireland car noise is not on anyone's agenda. Unlike some European cities, there is no attempt to measure overall noise levels. Although complaints to Dublin City Council's Air Quality and Noise Control Unit have been rising, they all focus on isolated forms of noise, from intruder alarms to open air concerts. The slow increase in ambient noise from traffic is not on their agenda, and simply tolerated by the city's inhabitants. Bizarrely, car noise probably increases car dependency: confronted by streets that are unpleasant to walk in, people are even more likely to climb into their car.

CARS AND HEALTH

While car transport allows people access to health facilities, it also has many negative health effects. Not only do car drivers impact on public health generally through the pollution and noise they cause, they also kill each other, their passengers and other people. Furthermore, it is now emerging that a car-based life-style is itself unhealthy.

In Ireland, 374 people died in road accidents in 2004. For decades car accidents have been a major cause of death in 'motorised' societies. The level of car accidents now has consequences for life expectancy generally. For example, car accidents are by far the leading cause of death for American youths aged fifteen to nineteen (Freund and Martin, 1993: 36). Indeed, Duany et al point out that in the USA, 'a child is twenty times more likely to die from an automobile mishap than from gang activity, as most young drivers are involved in *at least* one serious auto accident between ages sixteen and twenty' (Duany et al, 2001: 120). In terms of impact on public health, what matters is the overall level of fatalities, and in this context it is important to be clear that in most countries public policy has been successful, pushing *down* the overall level of fatalities despite the growing amount of car travel. Thus in the UK by the early 1990s fewer people were killed on the roads at any time since the 1920s (Erskine, 1996).

Similarly in the Greater Dublin Area road accident casualties fell sharply from 1998 to 2003. Despite this success car drivers are still killing each other and their passengers, and they also kill other people. For some time it has been suspected that making cars safer (first safety belts, now air bags) tends to encourage drivers to drive faster, so the risk is displaced onto pedestrians and cyclists (Peltzman, 1975). There is evidence from the UK that amongst pedestrians there is a straightforward relationship between social class and the risk of being hit by a car, and this is particularly so amongst children (Erskine, 1996). This seems to be partly because poorer people walk more, but mainly because they are more likely to live in areas with heavy traffic. However, overall pedestrian and even cyclist *fatalities* have been falling in the Greater Dublin Area. The problem is that to some extent this 'success' has been achieved by simply driving pedestrians – including children – off the streets. In the UK in 1971, 80% of parents were happy to see their seven to eight year olds walk to school on their own. By 1990, this figure had collapsed to 9% (Davis, 1992/3: 15).

The falling number of children who walk to school is symptomatic of the vicious circle of car dependency. Parents worry about their children's safety, so they drive their children to school. Consequently children lose the skills to use roads safely and at the same time there are now more cars on the roads, making the roads more dangerous. Once it becomes 'normal' for children to be driven to school, the distance between home and school increases, so that soon many children are living too far away from school to walk there.

Less walking as part of normal activity is one cause of rising levels of obesity. In Ireland as elsewhere, obesity levels are rising: over two thirds of adult men and just under half adult women are classified as overweight (with respectively 20% of men and 16% of women obese)[2]. On these measures Ireland is now one of the more obese countries of the EU (European Commission, 2005: 15), although obesity levels have not risen as fast or as high as in the UK and have not yet reached US levels. Obesity is now a major public health issue, contributing to coronary heart disease, stroke, some cancers, diabetes and depression (National Taskforce, 2005). In the USA inactive lifestyles are now considered to be second only to smoking as a cause of death in adults (Sallis et al, 2004).

For adults and children who want to ensure they do not get over-weight, the solution is to go to a gym – by car. A typical middle class gym has parking space for cars – and almost no bicycles. In many ways the gym is a technological fix for a problem that has been produced in part by our sedentary lifestyle, and one that itself involves high levels of car usage!

On the one hand we spend more time in the car, on the other hand we walk less. In particular, car-based suburbs may be seen as healthy, but in fact they are now part of a health problem. Taking exercise in a gym requires a special effort that may be difficult to sustain in the long term. By contrast, people who routinely walk around their neigh-bourhood to do the 'messages' – or even just to walk to the bus stop – are less likely to put on weight. There is already clear evidence that people who walk or cycle to work are healthier than those who use motorised transport (whether private car or public transport) (Sallis et al, 2004). American research now shows that obesity is related both to the amount of time people spend in their car, and the extent to which they live in low-density suburbs (Frank et al, 2004). It is quite probable that those who use public transport walk more on their journey to work than those who travel by private car, but this is not clear. What is clear is that car based suburbs are themselves *unhealthy*. This is because of two interlinked reasons. Firstly, routine destinations become further away and thus can only be reached by car, and secondly, the inhabitants use cars for short journeys of less than a mile that could be done on foot.[3]

CONCLUSION

The environmental case against the car is multi-dimension-al. Much of the damage that cars cause can be reduced or even eliminated without affecting the car itself. Thus some forms of damage (e.g. some exhaust emissions) can be eliminated by different technologies, and alternative fuels could eventually provide a solution for the car's destruction of non-renewable fuels. Other forms of environmental and health damage seem to be more inherent in car travel itself: cars require roads, which means they will use up land; where car ownership is widespread a car dependent lifestyle and its negative health impacts seem inevitable.

Probably both sets of arguments are simplistic. Technological fixes *can* restrain the car's environmental impact, but they are often outweighed by the sheer growth in car ownership and car usage. On the other hand, car ownership and car usage is much more variable than is acknowledged by simplistic diatribes against 'the car'. The car is going to be with us for a long time yet. The issue is how to ensure that it does not dominate us – or to put it another way, how car usage does not become car dependency.

Notes:

1 There are different base years for different countries and emissions, but in most cases the base year is 1990. The target years are between 2008 and 2012.

2 Figures based on the Body Mass Index (BMI) which is defined as weight (in kg) divided by height (in meters) squared. A BMI of 25 or more is considered overweight, 30 or more as obese.

3 And short car journeys lead to disproportionately high exhaust emissions.

Chapter 5

Transport and social exclusion: a city for everyone?

For many people, the main problem with Dublin's car dependency is the negative environmental consequences, consequences that affect everyone. By contrast, the consequences of Dublin's car dependency for social exclusion are rather different. Here there are clear winners and clear losers. Because car dependency has been built into the city, those who do not have access to a car are likely to lose out. This is particularly the case for those who have no choice in the matter, above all those who simply cannot afford a car. As this chapter shows, in a car dependent city, the car-less are marginalised.

THE DEMOCRATIC CAR?

From Henry Ford on, the great appeal of the car has been its democratic nature. As Gramsci (1971) pointed out long ago, Ford linked a particular form of production (the assembly line etc.) with a particular form of consumption ('mass consumption'). The car is the iconic artefact of the 20th century – in particular the second half – because both of the way it is (was) produced[1], and the way it is consumed. The car appeared to involve a classic trade off. The production of the car involved a loss of choice for the individual worker, since work became deskilled, fragmented and closely supervised, all to an unprecedented extent. By contrast, higher productivity ensured that workers could now buy cars, so consumption increased individual choice. The car enabled the worker – and hence putatively all members of society – to go anywhere. The car was democracy on wheels.

Before the car became a mass consumption good, there was some class-based opposition, since rich people in cars killed some poor people on foot (Albert, 1999). Once most people either had a car or could reasonably aspire to one, such opposition disappeared. In the epoch of the family car, the father-worker had priority access over the (house) wife. Even today, it is usually the case that women use public transport more than men, presumably because they do not have a car, and in older age cohorts, women are less likely than men to have a driving licence. However, the obvious solution to this gender inequality problem was *more cars* – one for him *and one for her*.

For a majority of adults in the West today, using a car is a *right*. Accessing this right involves obtaining a driving licence and then buying a car. The importance of this right for ordinary citizens is shown by the fact that in a study of 'critical moments' in the life history of UK adolescents, of 50 categories *none* involved voting or even politics in general, but two involved cars ('passing driving test' and 'getting a car') (Thomson et al, 2002). In other words, a significant aspect of the transition to young adulthood is now gaining access to what Mrs. Thatcher called approvingly 'The Great Car Society'.

Car ownership today is so widespread that it is often forgotten that many adults do not own their own car and must share with other members of their household. Some people (children, young teenagers) are too young to drive a car, while in an aging population there are increasing numbers of older people for whom driving is dangerous or frightening. And finally, there remain adults who simply cannot afford a car. When Hurricane Katrina hit New Orleans, most of the inhabitants had left – in their cars. Those without cars stayed. Given the total destruction of public transport in the USA, this was hardly surprising. In a car dependent society like the USA, those without cars are marginalised.

The issue here is not just poverty. It is whether poverty excludes people from normal society. One widely used definition of poverty is:

> [People are poor who...] lack the resources to obtain the type of diet, participate in the activities and have the living conditions which are customary, or at least widely recognised or approved, in the societies to which they belong (Townsend 1979: 31 quoted in Mingione 1996:8).

From this perspective, to be poor is to be unable to afford to be normal. Conversely, this concept of poverty suggests that the poor are not 'always with us'. It is perfectly possible for even the poorest to have incomes that allow participation in the society. In such a society there are of course inequalities, but also shared basic standards. What we can term *mobility exclusion* occurs when people's constrained physical immobility prevents them from participating in the normal activities of the society. Mobility *inclusion* suggests a definition of urban rights that include the right to mobility within the city. Such a right is even more to difficult to define ('how much mobility at what cost?') than the rights of social citizenship (Marshall, 1950) to education, training, housing and health, some of which are enshrined in declarations such as the Council of Europe's European Social Charter of 1961 and even the Social Chapter of the European Union. Nonetheless, the principle of the right to mobility is clear.

One crucial question is the extent to which such mobility requires a car. We have seen already that Dublin is a car dependent city. It is not simply that many people use cars. It is that people are constrained to use cars. On the one hand, the destinations to which they wish to travel are now widely dispersed. This is most obvious now in relation to employment, but also shopping, health facilities and entertainment, all of which are now dispersed across the Greater Dublin Area (Chapter 2). On the other hand, Dublin lacks an integrated transport system: at best one can travel from the suburbs to the city centre, but any other journey has to be made by car (Chapter 3). In this situation we can assume that those without a car will be severely disadvantaged, *in ways that they would not be in less car-dependent cities.* Furthermore, in this situation, since a car will be seen by people as a necessity, a car will be high on their list of possible expenditure. They will make sacrifices to own and run a car *which they would not make in a less car-dependent city.*

INCLUSION AND THE NEED FOR A PUBLIC TRANSPORT SYSTEM

Mobility exclusion therefore involves interaction between the inability to use a car (or the financial costs of owning one), the location of 'mobility sites' and the alternatives to using the car. Thus if sites are located close together they can be reached on foot, but this also depends on adequate and safe footpaths. Equally, sites that are relatively close can be reached by cycle, again especially if there are adequate cycle lanes. For many journeys in a city, however, public transport is the only alternative to the car. Investment in public transport can therefore make an important contribution to challenging social exclusion. However, this depends on seeing public transport as a system rather than as a series of independent routes.

An important issue here is the claim that individual transport investments disproportionately benefit the better off. In the 1980s this was one criticism of the Dublin DART line. How valid an argument is this against investment in public transport?

The most expensive investment in public transport is for high capacity railway lines that by definition require heavy usage to be even remotely profitable. The obvious routes are therefore lines that link affluent suburbs to the city centre. As the DART line shows, such lines can certainly entice commuters from their cars: in terms of reducing car usage they are an effective investment. The most systematic and extensive international comparisons (Kenworthy et al, 1997) show that the most cost effective way of ensuring a major modal shift on journeys to work (and hence of making mobility environmentally more sustainable) is the introduction of heavy rail services in *affluent* commuter areas.

Paradoxically, in car dependent cities it seems to be particularly the case that public transport benefits the rich. Thus the DART, Dublin's only major public transport investment in the second half of the 20th century, notoriously serves primarily the richer suburbs, especially on the south side of the city. In Athens the new metro project has a similar character. By definition, a car dependent city is one which lacks a public transport system and which therefore only invests in isolated prestige projects.

Such investments may well be criticised by economists' cost-benefit analysis, showing that public expenditure is being used to 'subsidise' the relatively affluent. The immediate problem here is that analysis that attempts to assess the differential social impact of transport investment almost inevitably focuses on individual routes. As Hodge (1995) has argued in his detailed discussion of such analysis in the USA, an over-focus on equity in relation to specific routes may well detract from the *general* benefits of public transport. In the UK social exclusion research has more recently attempted to use more sophisticated analysis to determine the costs and benefits of transport provision for different social groups (e.g. Social Exclusion Unit, 2002). Yet a cost benefit analysis at the level of a system as a whole is almost impossible, not least when no such system exists.

The more fundamental issue is that there are quite strong arguments for 'subsidising' the use of public facilities by the rich, since if the rich use public facilities they will use their political clout to ensure high standards. Indeed, it is a standard argument in social policy that public services such as public health and education need to be good enough to get the political support of the 'middle classes'. Of course, decades of research have also shown that those with high incomes gain more from state education than do the poor, not least because they have the knowledge and self-confidence to use the system to their full advantage. However, those who on 'equity grounds' draw the conclusion that public services should therefore be *marketised* produce a situation where the middle classes pay for their own 'social services' *and lose all interest in the standard of the services used by the population as a whole.* This produces a chicken-and-egg situation. If public medicine is bad, people buy private medicine, and thus have no interest in improving the public health system. Equally, if public transport is bad, people use their cars and lose interest in the standard of public transport. A public transport system will command little public support if, with the possible exception of a few isolated prestige projects, it has only a 'safety net' function for those who have no private car. Such a system will be locked into a vicious circle of declining resources, declining quality and declining passengers, and consequently further loss of political support. In transport, as in other areas of state provision, arguments that provision should be cost effectively targeted on specific groups have the (only sometimes unintended) corollary that such provision should be residual and second best.

PUBLIC TRANSPORT SYSTEMS AND LOCAL AREAS

An effective public transport system is precisely *a system*. Because it is not a series of discrete commuter routes, but a system linking all the areas of the city, it enables all citizens to move around their city. As we shall now see, the extent to which such a system exists has important impacts at local level. In particular, public transport can differentiate between areas that are in other ways very similar. In these terms it is particularly useful to compare Dublin and Helsinki. Unlike Athens and Bologna, they are both cities with a low population density (see also Chapter 1); in both cities working class and middle class suburbs are built on the same principles. However, as we have already seen, Dublin has been built as a car dependent city, whereas in Helsinki car dependency is restrained.

In the SceneSusTech project we compared Jobstown in Tallaght (Dublin) and Kontula in Helsinki. Both are peripheral suburban areas of social housing with high unemployment, their style typical for their respective country: Jobstown is semi-detached houses, Kontula apartment blocks. One major difference is the extent of public transport. While Dublin as a whole lacks any integrated transport system, the situation in Jobstown is particularly bad. One bus route links the area to the nearby Tallaght Town Centre which is the nearest large shopping facility 1.6km away; the bus also links to Dublin City Centre, itself several kilometres away. The bus shelters are often vandalised and indeed on occasions the service has been withdrawn because bus drivers have been attacked by local youths, and there are few local facilities within walking distance. In Kontula by contrast, there is a large shopping centre and a metro station; in the focus groups all participants considered this within walking distance. Certainly Kontula is hardly a tourist attraction: the metro station is just about clean, but bare and functional with some graffiti. Nonetheless, the area as a whole is well served by buses and in addition there is a so-called 'service-line' or smaller internal bus-line. Everybody lives within 500m of a bus stop, most within 250m. One metro stop away is Itäkeskus, a huge shopping come service centre, with all the main department stores and also all public facilities. And on the metro Kontula is only 17 minutes away from Helsinki city centre. If bad public transport and bad planning should exacerbate social exclusion, we should find this in Jobstown; if good public transport and integrated land use planning should reduce social exclusion, this should occur in Kontula.

In Dublin the SceneSusTech project also examined Clonskeagh as an example of a middle class suburb and Docklands as an inner city area undergoing 'gentrification'; in Helsinki these were matched with the middle class suburb of Länski-Pakila and the inner city area of Taka-Töölö. Both the Dublin and Helsinki middle class suburbs are housing areas that, like the American housing tracts they imitate, are essentially built for the car. Through traffic is segregated from local traffic and restricted to the boundaries of the housing area, beyond which the major roads are built on a scale which favours car commuting. Although Clonskeagh had the highest level of car usage of all twelve areas in our study, some public transport is available and the vast majority of those who travelled to work by car considered that could get to work by other means.[2] In Länski-Pakila public transport facilities were better and a significant number of people used the extensive walking and cycling routes. The impact of different quality public transport systems was clearly shown by the comparison between the two inner city areas. Residents of Taka-Töölö could and did use the extensive local tram and bus systems as well as the metro: car ownership and car usage were low. By contrast in the Dublin Docklands public transport usage was low, even amongst those who did not own a car: most people either drove or walked to work.

As we shall now see, the good transport links of Helsinki ensured that the inhabitants of Kontula were not excluded from the employment and recreational opportunities of Helsinki as a city. By contrast, in Jobstown those without a car were isolated: getting a job or even doing the shopping became major and sometimes insuperable logistical problems. Thus while actual car ownership is low in Jobstown, most people who do not have a car would buy one if only they could afford it. By contrast in Kontula, three quarters of those who did not own a car disagreed with the statement 'I would buy a car if only I could afford one'. In other words, in Jobstown the car is seen as a necessity, in Kontula the car is a (often desirable) 'luxury'.

MOBILITY EXCLUSION AND ACCESS TO EMPLOYMENT

The journey to work is the simplest starting point for a discussion on the different ways in which people use cars – and for what happens to those who do not have cars. Chapter 1 showed that overall Dublin has higher levels of travel to work by private car than many European cities (Figure 1.3). What does this mean for those that do not have cars?

To examine this we can use the results of the SceneSusTech project. We have already seen that Jobstown is car dependent, since there is bad public transport but reaching many facilities appears to require a car. This car dependency should create social exclusion since in Jobstown there are relatively many people who do not own a car. The implications of this combination of car dependency and low access to cars are highlighted by comparing Jobstown with other areas both of Dublin, where car dependency is built into the city and of Helsinki, where car dependency is more constrained.

In inner city Helsinki Taka-Töölö has the lowest level of travel to work by private car in the study (12%). As Figure

5.1 shows, it is also the area where the lowest proportion of car owners actually uses the car to travel to work (22%). Both Jobstown and Taka-Töölö have very low levels of car ownership, but for very different reasons. In Jobstown car ownership is low simply because of lack of resources: those who can afford a car will buy one. By contrast, in Taka-Töölö many people consider that their close location to the city centre, their good local facilities and the extensive public transport in the area all combine to ensure that they do not need a car.

Despite these large differences in the level of car usage, in both areas those who do use their car for work travel are very car dependent. In Taka-Töölö the few people who used their car had complicated journeys to work and often had to travel for work during the day. Thus one architect often had to visit different sites and had to use the car to carry large drawings and documents. For most people, however, even if they owned a car, walking, cycling or using public transport was more practical and more comfortable. In Taka-Töölö therefore, very few people use the car, and those who do, do so because their job depends on their car.

By contrast, in Jobstown considerably more people use the car to travel to work and the majority consider that they could in fact reach their employment by other means (public transport, on foot or by cycle). However, for a significant minority of them the car is clearly essential. Thus although the area has one of the lowest levels of car ownership in the study, it is the area where fully 92% of all car owners use their car to get to work – the highest proportion in the study (Figure 5.1). This suggests that in Jobstown the car is particularly important in order to access employment. Certainly most people's jobs are relatively close to home. Many women have cleaning jobs in the local office parks and Tallaght Hospital, men work in the industrial estates along the nearby motorways and these are particularly difficult to reach without a car.

Figure 5.1 Normal mode of travel to work, all employed aged 25-64, car owners

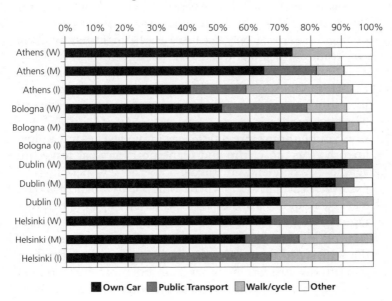

Source: *SceneSusTech survey*. Base: *All aged 25-64 and at work who own cars, N=212*

In Jobstown the car is seen as a necessity for access to employment. In the survey car owners were asked what problems would arise if they did not have a car; non-owners were asked the benefits they could imagine from having a car. In Jobstown 44% of owners mentioned employability as a potential problem, and 33% of non-owners mentioned employability – the highest area in the study.[3]

A quote from one of our interviews[4] documents what is involved, as well as showing the financial pressure of car ownership in low-income households:

Well we have always had a car, of one description or another, since we moved to Jobstown but I used to say so often that it was the biggest drain on our finances...We could live comfortably if we didn't have this car. And we had to have it, to live. And there was no alternative for him to get to work other than if he left the house at 6 o'clock in the morning to go all the way into town to come back out again to Lucan. Yet, if he had a car, he could go across that road in 15-20 minutes (Marie).

For men in Jobstown workplaces are normally the new factories and logistics centres along the M50 orbital motorway. These are relatively easy to reach by car from Jobstown, but using public transport would have involved taking a slow bus into the city centre and then another radial route out again.

In Kontula, however, virtually nobody who did not own a car mentioned access to employment as a possible advantage from car ownership. Not surprisingly therefore, Kontula had one of the lowest levels of car dependency for the journey to work in the study. It is safe to say therefore that in Kontula good public transport provision makes employment easy to access for those without cars and those on low incomes are not forced to buy a car in order to gain employment. Exactly the reverse operates in Jobstown: those without cars have added difficulties in getting a job, and those with cars are often making financial sacrifices for something that to them is expensive – but a necessity.

MOBILITY EXCLUSION AND ACCESS TO FACILITIES

In a car dependent city, not having a car creates problems and restricts people's potential activities. Just how bad this is depends on the nature of people's wants, where the facilities are located, and the shape of the public transport system. This affects education, shopping, entertainment, friendship and access to medical facilities – and the list is not exhaustive.

Travel to school

The survey asked how children in the household got to primary school. In Jobstown of the 29 respondents who had children at primary school, two thirds walked to school; in Clonskeagh only nine respondents reported children at primary school and of these all but one were driven to school in their parents' car. Part of the reason for this difference is simply that children in Clonskeagh are much less likely than children in Jobstown to go the nearest school to their house, and this is in fact particularly the case for secondary school.

Children are increasingly driven to school for two very different reasons. Firstly, parents consider that walking or cycling to school is unsafe. Paradoxically, the very fact that parents decide to drive their children to school makes roads less safe for children. More cars crowd onto the roads, facilities for pedestrians begin to wither, car drivers take less care for pedestrians. At the same time children lose the skills of using the roads, whether as pedestrians or as cyclists.

Secondly, parents are increasingly choosing the children's school, rather than simply sending their children to the nearest school. This is especially the case in Dublin where fee-paying schools have now become the norm for the suburban middle class in areas like Clonskeagh. Because children can be driven to school, the school can now be chosen from a wider geographical area. Explicit or implicit government policies that encourage parental 'choice' in education therefore increase the amount of car travel for children. At the same time, such an increase is likely to involve journeys that could not be made without a car. By contrast in middle class Länski-Pakila, children usually attend a local school and travel to school by bus or bicycle. For the middle class of Dublin, education involves car dependency in a way that does not in fact apply to working class parents or to middle class citizens of less car-dependent cities.

Shopping

Clonskeagh is motorised even for local shopping, although this activity is not strictly car dependent, since precisely one respondent in the survey felt that they had to use a car to do this shopping. Not surprisingly, nearly everyone in Clonskeagh used their car for shopping for large amounts of food. The situation is different in Jobstown, where only a quarter of people use a car for this, even though it is one of the journeys for which a car is most suitable. In the survey one person responded that they did this shopping on foot, but other people used the local bus service, got a lift in someone else's car, or used a taxi. At the time of study there were virtually no local shops in Jobstown[5] and with the supermarket hardly an easy walk away, large scale shopping can often be a major expedition. By contrast in Kontula, shopping facilities are not so far away and nearly half of the survey respondents reported that they did this shopping by foot – as did over half of the respondents in Taka-Töölö in inner city Helsinki. In a car dependent city like Dublin, even one of the most routine activities of contemporary life – doing the weekly shopping – becomes problematic for those who do not own a car: a situation which neatly fits the definition of social exclusion.

Visiting friends

In Jobstown more than in Clonskeagh social life is localised. At one stage in our study we asked focus group members to draw maps of their recent journeys: in Jobstown these were almost entirely within the area. According to our survey, in Jobstown most people's friends live in the immediate locality, but this is much less likely to be so in Clonskeagh; only a third of our Jobstown respondents used a car to visit friends, whereas this was the case for just under two thirds of our Clonskeagh respondents. Low car ownership in Jobstown almost certainly contributes to this localism, but this was not raised as a problem either in the survey or in the focus group. By contrast, they did feel constrained by the fact leisure facilities were so difficult to reach by public transport. Of all twelve areas in the study, people in Jobstown were most likely to report that facilities for hobbies and free-time pursuits were not within walking distance. As one put it:

> I would rarely, but I love to go to Clondalkin leisure centre. But it is just not accessible from here. Now and again on a Saturday or a Sunday, we'd go in the car or that. But I would love at 6 o'clock in the evening or so when the dinner is all over and that to go off out and say I'm going to the thing – but it is just not possible to do that because of transport. Do you know what I mean? (Marie)

Medical facilities

In Jobstown there is a doctor's surgery within walking distance of most people, but for medical emergencies people need cars. So as Marie explains, neighbours with cars are thus a valuable resource in times of medical and maternity needs:

> If children get sick in the night time...You don't get a doctor out here in the night time. Once surgery is closed, that's it. For that reason it is vital that someone in the area would have a car so that you could go to a neighbour and ask them if they did not mind etc. It has happened us a fair bit and people would knock. Especially now going to the maternity ward. My husband has been mistaken for being the father a fair few times because often her [the expectant mother's] husband would have to stay at home with the other kids.

In Jobstown, unlike in more middle class areas, access to private transport has a gender dimension. Many single mothers cannot afford a car at all; where women are living with a husband or partner, it is often he who uses the car most. Sometimes women don't know how to drive and are reluctant to learn; often the additional expense of insurance makes driving prohibitive. Interestingly, while women in Kontula were also less likely to drive than men, and while women in Kontula also lived localised lives, the interviews did not produce any sense of frustration: car driving was seen as an unnecessary expense, rather than something that they wished they had the courage or the money to be able to do.

In many ways, a car is essential in Jobstown even if you don't have one. Accordingly, not having a car excludes people from some aspects of normal life in a way that does not occur to those without cars in Kontula. Asked what problems they would face if they did not have a car, car-owners in Jobstown reeled off a list of issues: getting a job, socialising, seeing dependents and going to the shops (Table 5.1a). In Kontula by contrast, the only serious problem car owners considered they would have was 'going to country'. Indeed, in Kontula many cars are, in the Finnish expression, 'summer cars' – cars that are not maintained through the winter and only used in the summer, in particular for excursions to the countryside. Equally, Kontula residents who do not have a car consider 'going to the country' the most important possible benefit of car-ownership (Table 5.1b). This contrast shows how in Kontula, car ownership is not a necessity because the city is not car dependent; in Jobstown car ownership is a necessity because Dublin is car dependent – and those without a car pay an additional penalty.

Table 5.1a Problems car owners would face
if did not own a car

(Percentage of car owners mentioning each possible problem)

Area	Employ-ment	Sociab-ility	Seeing depen-dents	Shop	Going to country	Other	None
Dublin (W)	44	44	31	25	0	69	13
Dublin (M)	19	28	22	19	0	78	17
Dublin (I)	23	46	0	39	0	54	0
Helsinki (W)	5	16	0	0	69	11	16
Helsinki (M)	14	21	0	11	39	21	18
Helsinki (I)	17	17	0	11	67	28	6

Source: *SceneSusTech survey.* Base: *car owners only*

Table 5.1b Gains for non-car owners if had a car

(Percentage of non-car owners mentioning each possible benefit)

Area	Employ-ment	Sociab-ility	Seeing depen-dents	Shop	Going to country	Other	None
Dublin (W)	33	14	61	11	0	56	8
Dublin (M)	8	0	31	0	0	31	39
Dublin (I)	17	6	86	11	0	33	3
Helsinki (W)	4	21	0	4	25	33	38
Helsinki (M)	0	0	0	0	42	8	58
Helsinki (I)	8	35	0	15	58	23	15

Source: *SceneSusTech survey.* Base: *non-car owners only*

SOCIAL CITIZENSHIP AND PUBLIC TRANSPORT

Jobstown is not unique and not the most deprived area of
Dublin. There are other areas of suburban Dublin with

similar levels of unemployment and poverty. In terms of mobility, the problem for the people of areas like Jobstown is not that relatively few of them own cars; the problem is that many cannot afford a car in a city that is designed for cars.

To some extent focusing on areas with concentrations of poverty such as Jobstown under-estimates the extent of 'mobility exclusion'. Poverty researchers have argued that the focus on 'deprived areas' (such as Jobstown) under-estimates the extent of poverty across the society as a whole: many if not most poor people do *not* live in 'poor' areas (e.g. Nolan et al, 1999). In terms of mobility there are even some advantages in living in a poor area, since as we have seen, here people develop ways of sharing resources (e.g. the neighbour who gives a lift in a medical emergency) and many friendship patterns are localised – social ties are maintained without extensive mobility. Those people who are poor in areas where the risk[6] of poverty is lower have less access to such forms of self-help. In the older inner suburbs of the city public transport does exist: we have seen that even affluent and car-rich Clonskeagh does have some public transport facilities. As Dublin spreads out beyond the M50, suburbs are being built where public transport is minimal and the distance to employment and facilities increases. This new suburbanisation is creating a situation where the car is an absolute necessity for normal life. In such areas to be poor is to face extremes of mobility exclusion.

Mobility exclusion affects not just the poor but also the young and the old. In Dublin the senior citizens' pass allows them free (off peak) public transport, but this is of little use if such public transport does not exist. Equally, weak public transport means that young people try to acquire a car as young as possible, since without one their social life is restricted. Given that car accidents and especially fatalities are highest among young people, we have the bizarre situation that public policy de facto pushes young people towards car ownership – and the risk of death – as fast as possible.

Mobility inclusion therefore requires an effective public transport system. It also requires that people's transport destinations are within reach of public transport and that facilities are as far as possible localised. In Dublin today the trend is in the opposite direction. Employment is increasingly in new suburban office parks and industrial estates with minimal public transport; shopping is in large suburban retail parks where non-car owners are barely tolerated (Chapter 2).

Such an understanding of public transport and social inclusion seems very far from much policy discussion in Dublin today. Thus a study commissioned by the Public Transport Partnership Forum (NERA and TIS.PIT, 2001) reviewed public transport in Dublin compared with Adelaide, Copenhagen, Evora, Lyon, Manchester, Preston, The Hague, Toronto and Zurich. Yet even this report, despite an explicit attempt to get beyond an evaluation in terms of narrow economic efficiency, merely defined 'inclusion' as the extent to which transport facilities were accessible to the disabled: conventional issues of inequality or social class were literally not mentioned[7].

In a car dependent city like Dublin, one solution to mobility exclusion might be simply to ensure that everyone who wants a car should be able to buy one. It could be argued that this would recognise the reality – that outside the city centre housing and employment is now simply too dispersed to be serviced properly by public transport; it would recognise the importance of the car in contemporary social life. And furthermore it could be argued that now, unlike even twenty years ago, the overall increase in living standards means that at a poverty line of 60% of the median income it is realistic for everyone to be able to afford a car: a cheap Ford rather than a BMW, but a car nonetheless. In practical policy terms this would require a policy objective of keeping car prices as low as possible, especially for the cheapest models (e.g. by low car tax on low powered cars) and ensuring that running a car is as cheap as possible (again most obviously through taxation).

Such a policy has the obvious advantage that it avoids the charge of elitism that is often levelled at environmentalist critics of 'hyper mobility' (e.g. Urry, 2002). Yet however superficially attractive it may be, such a vision of what Margaret Thatcher termed 'the Great Car Society' is hardly socially progressive. It ignores the environmental consequences of increased car use, and Chapter 4 has already shown that these can at most only be mitigated by technological fixes such as different fuels. Increased car usage is not neutral for those who do not use cars, since the more people who use cars, the more difficult it is for those who do not – and the pressure on them to switch increases. At the same time, the charge of elitism is misplaced: it is often the affluent who live in areas that are well serviced by local facilities and by public transport (e.g. inner city Helsinki, or even Manhattan in New York) who are able to choose not to use a car. The populist solution appears to allow people choice, but in fact ensures that the vast majority have *no* choice. And of course it does nothing for those who are too young or too old to drive.

The argument that mass auto-mobility is required to ensure social inclusion is inadequate. It is impossible to fulfil everyone's basic mobility needs through private transport, and so accepts as 'realistic' the marginalisation of the poor, the old and the young. The claim that cars are now 'necessary' for everyone because commercial interests have created spaces that can only be connected by private transport, accepts a particular urban configuration as somehow natural and inevitable. Empirical research can show that the extent to which such car dependence occurs is itself variable and not the inevitable result of 'economic growth', 'globalisation' or any other allegedly universal social trend. Cities can still in some sense *choose* whether or not to be car dependent.

Notes:

1   Studies of car plants occupied a key role in the 'industrial sociology' of the second half of the 20th century. Car workers were at the centre of attention in the 1960s with the 'affluent worker' debate; car plants at the centre of the 'Japanisation'; and 'lean production' debates of the 1990s. In Germany debates over 'polarisation' in the 1970s were followed in the 1990s by debates over 'reprofessionalisation', again focusing on car plants. By contrast the sociology of the car as transport was largely abandoned to cultural studies. For literature review see Wickham et al (2002), Chapter 1.

2   This was true even though the study was carried out shortly before the local QBC (Quality Bus Corridor) was introduced.

3. Open ended questions; multiple choices coded.

4. In these quotations all names are pseudonyms; for full accounts of the focus groups see Rajanti (2002). The Dublin report was compiled by Maria Lohan; the Helsinki report by Taina Rajanti.

5   Today the situation has improved slightly with several small shops and a Londis supermarket in the area.

6   Researchers distinguish between the risk of poverty, i.e. the likelihood of being poor in a particular area, and the incidence of poverty, i.e. the share of poor people from that area within the total population.

7   Intriguingly, this narrow understanding seems to be common where public transport is weak. Thus in the SceneSusTech project, it was also the understanding of social inclusion put forward by the Greek experts in relation to Athens, another city with a weak public transport system.

Chapter 6

Car dependency and the quality of urban life

Two images present the future of Dublin. On the one hand, Dublin the living city, a city in which people meet each other, a city of urban life, a city with a clear identity based around its public spaces and a distinctive streetscape. This is Dublin as a quintessentially European city. On the other hand, Dublin as metro-land, a city region sprawling out across Eastern Ireland, a city with no centre, a place that is a 'no place' but which suspiciously resembles Los Angeles. In the former the city is tied together by its public transport, in the latter by its motorways.

In the film 'Crash' set in Los Angeles a character remarks that in a normal city you meet people in the street, in LA you crash into each other in your cars. A city that is car dependent involves not just a particular spatial configuration but also a reduced quality of life, and above all, the destruction of the potentiality of city living. This is a question of *social cohesion*, that is to say, the ability of people who do not know each other personally to live together in a trusting and civilised way. Whereas issues of inclusion effect only the marginalised, questions of cohesion affect everyone. At its most mundane urban cohesion is about the safe and even pleasurable use of public space; at its most grandiose it is a question of urban citizenship. Social cohesion is the quality of urban life, the extent of social trust and the quality of personal interaction in the world beyond our homes and workplaces. Outside in the city, do we experience people we do not know as fellow citizens or as threatening strangers?

Today more people are buying cars than ever before, but a long tradition of urban design sees this as reprehensible. The architectural and even aesthetic critique of the car in the city predates our more recent concerns with the environmental and ecological impact of the car. It is easy to denigrate this approach as elitist, and the car-based city has its enthusiastic proponents who can usually claim to be realists. As we shall now see, such populism ignores the fact that car dependency undermines the quality of life for everyone. Conversely, effective public transport contributes to the quality of urban life. However, while car dependency definitely destroys cities, improved public transport is not a magic bullet that on its own revives them. Critics of the car often ignore the concerns of transport users about public safety: creating urban citizenship requires *safe* public transport. If this is achieved, then public transport becomes a crucial part of the public realm of our cities, a component of a genuine citizenship.

Car usage and the dying city

Forty years ago in the USA, when the inter-state highway system was completed, when car-based suburbanisation had been developing for twenty years, American cities began to be improved: slum neighbourhoods were torn down and new urban freeways bulldozed through the old ethnic quarters. In that optimistic age, Jane Jacobs' book *The Life and Death of American Cities* was an apparently quixotic counterblast (Jacobs, 1962). While planners and developers tried to segregate land uses (so-called 'functional zoning'), Jacobs praised messy multi-functional usage; while developers built suburbs in which everyone had a car, Jacobs praised the inner city pedestrian neighbourhood; where developers wanted to create more private space for living, Jacobs defended public space. From Jacobs, today's 'new urbanism' movement has inherited the insight that car dependency and the quality of urban life are incompatible.

Cars and the destruction of public space

For Jacobs what mattered about a city was the street, or more particularly, the pavement ('sidewalk'). Pavements are used to walk somewhere, to reach a place or to meet a person, but they are also used just for strolling and for hanging out, they can develop stools or chairs and become places to sit. The pavement is a public place – anyone can use it, and they do not have to account for what they are doing. For Jacobs the curious point about pavements in busy neighbourhoods is that they are safe – people watch over each other. In her famous phrase, 'there are eyes on the street'.

Such defensible public space depends upon being used by different types of people. Hence, Jacobs' enthusiasm for the small local shop, the small local business, the variety of local housing. Her conception of the urban neighbourhood is very different to the village community where everyone knows everything about everybody. The attraction of the city has always been the escape from such a valley of squinting windows. In the urban neighbourhood some people recognise each other, some people know something about some other people, but privacy is respected. For that reason, according to Jacobs, diversity is tolerated in a way that it is not in more tight-knit communities. Equally, the pavement is public space on which people of different ages, classes and ethnic groups all meet – they do not go into each other's houses, but they do have to behave with respect to each other on the street. The urban neighbour-hood is an example of the 'strength of weak ties', or to use another fashionable sociological term, 'social capital'. Such weak ties can ensure that parks and playgrounds do not become dangerous and threatening spaces – they are used and hence we might say 'policed' by different groups of people.

An obvious problem with Jacobs' argument is that it appears to treat the city as at most a network of villages. However, the city is an entity of a different scale than a neighbourhood: at the level of the city most people are con-tinually interacting with people they do not know at all. Here too the idea of public space is important, but the social relations on which it depends are far more anony-mous than in the neighbourhood. The city depends on civilised relations between strangers if its public places and public pavements are to be used. The sociologist Richard Sennett has described how from the 18th century onwards, the growing European city became a place of strangers, yet a place in which strangers 'knew' how to meet each other. The word city is of course linked to citizen, but also to 'civility': how to share public space with strangers. At its most fundamental then, the promise of the city is the chance to be different, to be individual, but at the same time to trust the stranger (Sennett, 2002).

Such ideas are part of the new urbanism that is today promoted by many planners and architects such as Richard Rogers. For them the key issue is to create public multi-used space. Reiterating a point stressed by Jacobs, Rogers argues that 'open-minded' spaces are 'multi-functional'. The car park, the shopping mall and the motorway all serve only one function. By contrast public spaces ('the busy square, the lively street, the market, the park, the pavement café') serve many functions: they are places where 'we are readier to meet people's gaze and participate' (Rogers, 1997: 9). These arguments make one think immediately of the city centre, but in the USA in particular the new urbanism is trying to create or even redesign suburbs on the same principles (Katz, 1994).

However, such multi-functional public spaces are difficult to create in a car dependent city. If cities are built for cars, then they are hostile to people. Cars take up space that pedestrians could use, they even push pedestrians away. When roads are widened to give more space to cars, pedestrians end up with less space or even none at all. All motorways and many dual carriageways have no pavements, as indeed do the roads in many American suburbs – just as on a motorway, anyone walking is likely to be stopped by a cruising police car. In such circumstances, the shared public space of the citizen has been removed.

On a larger scale, functional zoning segregates uses into different areas, so different activities (living, shopping, working, etc) all become physically separated from each other – and then connected by car. By contrast, in an urban neighbourhood people live, work and shop within the same area, and can reach these different sites on foot. Furthermore, the neighbourhood is inhabited by different types of people. In some districts of 19th century European cities different people lived in the same houses, segregated not by area but by floor – the poor lived in the attic storeys (lots of stairs, cold in winter, hot in summer), the better off in the more spacious lower floors. Alternatively, the poorer inhabitants of the block might live in the backyard (the German 'Hinterhof'), the better off over the shop at the front. Even today, some areas of cities continue to be home to very different social strata, who all share the same pavements, the same shops and even perhaps the same pub or café.

Such multiple use neighbourhoods were the exception rather than the rule. Jacobs was describing something that was hardly normal even when she was writing. The growth of 19th century cities, whether in Europe or the USA, was a process whereby home and work were increasingly separated, first for the middle class and then for the working class. This does not invalidate her argument: mid 20th century cities based on the automobile regarded as reprehensible the social arrangements that made city life rewarding and its public spaces safe. Conversely, American suburbia epitomises the destruction of public space – not least because it is based on the car. Is Dublin heading in the same direction?

Cars and the creation of private space
The expansion of private car usage is an expansion of private space. With cars the expansion of the individual's private space has negative impact on public space. At its most general, a car-based society tends to be individualistic. Furthermore, a car-based society tends to homogenise space, making somewhere into anywhere.

Some people, especially perhaps younger people, enjoy driving, just as notoriously cars are status symbols or even sexual symbols. However, unlike many other forms of ostentatious consumption, the car impacts on other people in ways that expensive jewellery or clothes do not. Thus the sudden fashion in Ireland for SUVs is not just a question of display; it is also indicates a desire to wall oneself off from the grubby and threatening multitude outside. Today, when SUVs are ubiquitous and derivatives of the US Army armoured Humvee are sold as private cars in the USA, Jacobs was remarkably prescient: she described one response to unsafe streets as people 'hiding in their cars...like tourists in the game reserves of Africa' (Jacobs, 1962: 46). People on the pavement, just like users of public transport, are not exercising this option: they are compelled to share space with strangers.

SUVs' fuel consumption is not justified by any utilitarian argument and they wilfully contribute to global warming with higher emissions. The desire to barricade oneself off from the rest of the world means a car that is particularly dangerous to other road users. Thus SUVs are more likely to cause injury when involved in an accident than other cars. Similarly, when culturally challenged young men drive around playing music on their sound systems which are designed to make noise outside the car, they are only parodying the 'carcooned' behaviour of more responsible adults, who, wrapped in their world of metal, are oblivious to the impact of their behaviour on the outside world.

In a consumerist society, criticism of others' pleasures is not really socially acceptable. For example, we might claim that if young men want to kill themselves in cars, then ultimately that is their responsibility, at least if they have not stolen the car. Car 'accidents', however, indicate the general problem. Car drivers often kill other people as well, ranging from their passengers to other drivers and pedestrians. Individuals' right to cars can sometimes comes at a very high cost for the rest of society.

Anti-social behaviour, such as joyriding, driving SUVs while sober or clapped out bangers while drunk, can in principle be constrained by law. There are, however, much more fundamental and much more insidious implications of extensive car usage for social cohesion. Nothing expresses better the individualism of the car than the simple fact that the average American now spends more than one hour a day driving. The average of 72 minutes is about twice as much as the average American parent spends with their child (Putnam, 2000: 212). At the centre of this travel is the daily commute. According to the census, 12% of all commuters in Dublin City and County took over an hour to get to work in 2002, a figure that rises to over 20% in the three outer counties of the Greater Dublin Area. According to one study of work-life balance issues which compared Dublin with Bologna, Copenhagen and Paris, Dublin commuters spent the most time on the journey to work (39 minutes) and those in Bologna the least (24 minutes). These figures are probably on the low side. From the SceneSusTech survey those who travelled to work by car in Dublin spent on average 1.8 hours in the car on a normal working day. In Dublin the impact of long hours in the car are exacerbated by long working hours, at least for men: in the work life balance study, Dublin *men* also had the longest working hours (45 hours per week, compared with 42 in the study as a whole) (Fine-Davis et al, 2004: 134).

These long hours in the car occur because the journey to work is only one of the regular journeys people make. It is often combined with dropping children off at crèche or school and indeed, this is now one of the ways parents manage to spend time with their children. Yet Americans do not only ' bowl alone', they also drive alone: the car is increasingly used alone, at least for the journey to work. In the USA vehicle occupancy is falling (Putnam, 2000: 212), and in Ireland car *passengers* as a proportion of those travelling to work fell between 1996 and 2002 from 10% to 7% of the total. Interestingly, however, the SceneSusTech survey showed that in the Dublin areas covered by our own survey, around one half of car drivers had a passenger for at least some part of their journey to work.

As our different sites of activity become more separated from one another, we spend more time simply moving between them. The journey to work is only one side of what Putnam calls the 'triangle' of movement between home, work and the shopping mall. For Putnam, car-based suburbanisation is a major cause of the decline in social capital. Its key impact is simply in terms of time: there is plentiful evidence that people who have long commuting time are less likely to spend time on 'civic engagement' in local voluntary associations etc. In addition, like many other American commentators, Putnam argues that the increasing social segregation of American suburbs itself means that suburbanites may be concerned about their own small community, but have less and less concern for the wider society.

At the moment the extent to which Dublin's spreading suburbs resemble those of the US Sunbelt is still unclear. Some studies show high levels of social engagement in these areas (Peillon et al, 2006). Yet this may just be an effect of novelty, for US data shows high level of community involvement in the 1960s suburban expansion, but a decline thereafter. And the obstacles to community life are enormous. Where both partners are working full-time, suburbs have to become dormitories – it was after all the much-maligned suburban housewife who kept alive the local chains of gossip and the local parent teacher association. Where there are children, parents are likely to return to work as early as possible for financial reasons, not least because of Ireland's limited support for parental leave.

In fact Dublin's outer suburbs are now beginning to show signs of the social segregation that is endemic in the USA where 80% of all new developments are now 'gated communities' (Blakely and Snyder, 1997; Luymes, 1997). Gated communities surrounded by their own security perimeter are an extreme case of the destruction of public space. When the outside world is seen as threatening, more and more people (and not just the very rich) opt to hire their own security guards, while the poor respond by seeking safety in the protection racket and the gangland turf. While gated communities do reduce crime within their boundaries, studies also show they lead to a collapse of citizenship and of broader civic engagement (Lang and Danielson, 1997). We have not yet reached this situation in Ireland, but there are symptoms. Builders are tending to build larger and more homogenous developments, so that the social mix on any one development is quite narrow, quite apart from the fact that the social housing provision remains effectively a dead letter.

All of this means that the home is an isolated private space, with little connection to any broader public realm. This is even clearer in the case of shopping which increasingly occurs in privatised shopping centres and shopping malls. To the extent that these have no connection to any effective public transport, they inevitably create car journeys. To the extent that they are walled off private space, they replace public space. Even if Dundrum is connected to the Luas, the shopping experience is privatised in a way that it is not in the City Centre. The shopping centre may provide an ersatz 'piazza' in which people do meet each other and just hang out but this comes at the cost of a deterioration in the quality of public space outside. Instead of all participating in common space, for which therefore all are responsible, the undesirable are kept outside – and ignored.

While the public space of Dublin's city centre has been enhanced, in the suburbs roads become sewers instead of meeting places, unoccupied by people as the cars whiz by. Roads become transmission belts for private cars moving between one private space and another. Every now and then, outer Dublin already resembles South Africa, where roads slice through danger zones to connect the private safe spaces of the affluent. Of course we are not there yet, but it's worth asking which is closer to Dublin, the Los Angeles resident in his fortified SUV travelling from private shopping mall to gated community, or the Italian strolling out for the evening passagiata in the public square. For ultimately that is the contrast. As private spaces multiply and public spaces decline, the great European legacy of the city as a public realm wilts. As an American critic such as James Kunstler points out, this car-based landscape becomes a 'geography of nowhere' (Kunstler, 2004). Our physical environment becomes more homogenous; we may be travelling more, but there is less sense of going from somewhere to somewhere else. In John Updike's recent novel, a character looks back over his years in East Coast villages and describes it as having occurred in somewheres that are becoming anywheres. Welcome to Dublin?

URBAN DESIGN AND URBAN TRANSPORT

Putting people back on the streets

According to the new urbanist orthodoxy, planning and urban design should no longer facilitate the car, but instead empower the pedestrian. City centres should be places within which people can *walk*. In the area where they live, people should be able to meet immediate needs from facilities that are within walking distance. Finally, people should be able to reach major destinations without using a private car.

Across Europe, the first of these objectives is often achieved. Unlike in most American cities, the centres of many large European cities have not collapsed. They have been kept attractive by public investment, which has enabled them to co-exist with new out of town shopping centres. Central to this has been curbing the car and facilitating pedestrians. In Copenhagen for example, the planners put as much street furniture (benches, chairs etc) as possible onto the streets, ensuring that they are difficult for cars to use. It is easy to deride this as meaning just lots of café bars, but policies like this have for the moment at least rescued Dublin's key shopping areas, ensuring that the city is now participating in a Europe-wide revival of city centres.

In a city the size of Dublin, public transport can play a key role, since it can *extend the area of the pavement city*. If there is a dense network of public transport in the city centre, then the area that people can walk around extends dramatically. This is not public transport as delivering people *to* the city centre; it is transport so that people can move themselves around *within* the city centre, which in the process becomes larger. In a city like Paris or London, this role is played by the Metro or the Underground. In cities that are closer to the size of Dublin, it is often played by the tram. If trams are easy to use, with very frequent stops, easy ticketing and clear route maps, the tram can become almost a moving pavement, something that you jump on and off almost at will. It is even suggested that since the tramlines are visible in the road, pedestrians are more likely to wait for a tram than for a bus! Because they are above ground, trams are visible to pedestrians; because the passengers look out, trams put eyes back on the street. With good design trams can enhance the urban fabric. In Australia, Melbourne's trams are now a symbol of the city – not least as they move slowly down the city's smartest and pedestrianised shopping streets.

If Luas means 'speed' in Irish, it is perhaps odd to think of it as slowly moving street furniture. Trams, however, can play two rather different roles. In the first role, the tram as a moving pavement, they move around a small area. In this case, as in many European cities, they have to be part of the street. Stops are small, informal and do not intrude into the cityscape; catenaries (the poles and overhead wires) are equally non-intrusive and wires are often attached to buildings rather than on poles. Passengers only travel short distances, and because they are on the street, they can see where they are going. Passengers are travelling through the city and feel part of it.

In its second role, the tram can be understood as a cheap railway, as a modernised suburban railway, as 'light rail'. Here, tracks are segregated completely from roads and so speeds can be as high as on a suburban train; because of the higher speeds the tram requires railway-type signalling, but visual intrusion into the cityscape is not an issue. Journeys are longer, stops are less frequent, and the routes are usually from suburb to city centre and designed mainly for commuting.

To some extent these different conceptions of the tram are a contrast between Continental Europe and the UK (and even the USA). Especially in Germany and Austria, trams survived after the war, as they did in cities as different as Porto and Sarajevo. The revival of the tram in France has built on this heritage: the new French trams in Nantes, Grenoble, Strasbourg etc. have consciously been built as part of a political project to reduce car traffic and at the same time enhance the urban environment, including its visual element. In the UK by contrast, 'light rail' has been conceived as the solution to a transport problem – how to improve the link between the suburbs and the city centre. Furthermore, they have been judged by very tight financial targets, with the usual British obsession of increasing the role of the private sector and minimising public expenditure (Hylen and Pharaoh, 2002). French urban planners see the tram in terms of urban design; British transport planners see the tram in terms of cost-effectiveness. While Manchester's tram makes the city centre look even more ugly, Montpellier's tram enhances a beautiful city.

The strength of the modern tram is that of course it can play both roles, and to a large extent Dublin's Luas does. Thus the Green Line from Sandyford is for most of its journey an up-market suburban train, running as it does along the old Harcourt Street Line track bed. Descending from the viaduct at Charlemont Bridge, however, it becomes part of the city, just as the Tallaght–Connolly Station line does for its final stage from Heuston Station into town. In its city centre sections, the overhead lines are usually fixed to buildings and where there are poles they are not visually intrusive. The success of Luas as urban design can be seen from the fact that already it features on Dublin postcards. It looks nice from the outside and, at the same time, it makes the city look nice from the inside. As one enthusiastic journalist wrote on the Luas's first birthday:

'Last Monday, as the Luas crossed O'Connell Street, the nation's main thoroughfare at least had the semblance of the handsome, evocative boulevard it should be.' (Doyle, 2005).

However, it is clear that Luas was planned primarily as a UK style light rail, facilitating the commute from suburb to city centre. Even joining up the two lines, as is now finally planned, is still conceptualised in terms of facilitating relatively long journeys. By contrast, the plan floated by Dublin City planner Dick Gleeson to create a 'figure of eight' line by running a line along Dame Street and Pearse Street, linking across the river both at O'Connell Bridge and at the Point Depot, would tie together Dublin's city centre. As Gleeson remarked, with this system it would be possible for people working in the IFSC to have lunch in Phoenix Park (Irish Times, 25.05.2004). At the moment by contrast, in most areas of the inner city people only use public transport to leave the city.

For American planners and architects of the new urbanism, a key slogan has been 'Transit Oriented Development', designing living areas that both reduce the need for car-based local journeys and facilitate residents using 'transit' (i.e. public transport) for longer journeys, especially to the city centre. Within the housing area this means higher housing densities, good local facilities, priority for pedestrians and cyclists. Rather than widening streets, planners try to narrow them, often by blocking them with parked cars. In the USA this meant a call for a return to what Americans called the 'street car suburb', where activity such as shops clustered around local tram stops. Again, Luas is already partly achieving this, with new small shops opening at several stops on the Green Line. At the same time, the area should be well served by public transport, so that people can reach more distant destinations without using a car.

Whether people walk or cycle *within* their neighbourhood can be influenced by the design of the neighbourhood itself (Cevero and Radisch, 1996). Thus SceneSusTech discovered that middle class suburbs in Dublin and Helsinki, though superficially both based on the private car, also show some significant differences in the nature and use of public space. Even in the same broadly similar physical surroundings, Dubliners avoid public spaces more than their Finnish counterparts. Thus, in Clonskeagh what strikes one, according to our ethnographic reports, is 'the quietness of it all', whereas in Länsi-Pakila 'there are people walking – kids and adults'. The physical layout of Länsi-Pakila facilitates cycling and walking in a way that Clonskeagh does not. In Clonskeagh the main roads around the area frequently have no cycle lanes or even footpaths, thus discouraging cycling and walking outside the immediate estates, although within the estates there are adequate footpaths and traffic is calmed by speed ramps. In Länsi-Pakila by contrast, roads around the area, even though busy, have well kept pedestrian/bicycle lanes. Within the area there are often pedestrian/bicycle gravel lanes that traverse the area almost completely within woods. Even in the Finnish winter many are swept clean and all are in use. Accordingly, in Länsi-Pakila the physical layout facilitates those who wish to walk or cycle, thus creating small-scale public mobility spaces, whereas in Clonskeagh, despite the milder climate, the car is the only mode of transport that is facilitated.

Within the Council area, Dublin City Council planning is now committed to new urbanist principles: it aims to increase housing densities and lower car usage. Clearly, new urbanist principles have more immediate relevance in the city area than in the newer low-density suburbs. However, the Council faces the paradox that most people still believe car ownership is essential, which forces it to insist that new housing has off-street parking. There is a vicious circle here. Because there is such weak public transport within the city area, people still need a car to move around, although for these short journeys many use taxis which are now a vital part of public transport within the city. However, if car usage is to be restrained within the city area as a whole, it will be necessary to improve public transport in the older inner suburbs and to ensure that the new housing areas of the inner city, such as the Docklands, are connected to a transport grid. The original DTO transport plan foresaw a relatively dense network of Luas and Metro lines within the City, with for example a Luas line from the city centre to Dundrum via Terenure and one to the Point Depot from Dolphin's Barn. Such a grid pattern would have ensured that Dublin City would have become as accessible by public transport as the centre of Paris. Although this vision of the city now seems to have been quietly abandoned by transport planners, a dense public transport net could revive Dublin as a pavement city.

On the largest scale, new urbanist principles assert that all activity sites should be reached by public transport. Ideally, if something can only be reached by private car, it should not be built. For large-scale developments this means of course that shopping centres should be on public transport. In Helsinki for example the largest shopping centre in Scandinavia at Itäkeskus is built around a stop on the new metro line. In Dublin the Dundrum shopping centre is on the Luas, but in fact this is the only such centre that has effective public transport – and Dundrum's scale means that most people in its catchment area can only reach it by private car. Nonetheless, Dundrum, like the Luas as a whole, shows that large-scale private development can be profitably linked to public transport. Once public transport links effectively the main destinations people could wish to reach within the city area, the pedestrian is empowered. On the one hand the pedestrian can explore the city by transport, but on the other hand the pedestrian walks to the nearest transit stop, thus again putting people back onto the streets.

Mobility knowledge and public space

Part of living in the city is to know one's way around it. For most people this means using a car, and car driving involves therefore not just the knowledge of driving the car but the knowledge of where things are and how they are to be found. In our focus groups people in Dublin and Athens in particular stressed that knowing how to drive also meant knowing how to avoid congested times and routes and knowing where to park. Car drivers have a 'mental map' of the city as formed by its roads.

Public transport users have different mobility skills and a different map – one formed by the transport routes. The precursor of all such maps was London Transport's Underground map first published in the 1930s. Famously this is a 'schema'; it is not in fact a map in the sense of being to scale. Its designer, Eric Gill, placed points where they would make sense to the map-reader, not as a direct scale copy of their position on a normal map. Yet far better than any scale map, the plan of the Underground allows Londoners and visitors to orient themselves and to move around. Learning to understand such a transport map is one crucial mobility skill for public transport users, just as are the skills of knowing how to use a bus (where to pay, how to get on and off etc), and the practical knowledge of when buses and trains are likely to arrive.

Not surprisingly, in Lanski-Pakila in Helsinki young people have more what we could term 'mobility skills' than their counterparts in Clonskeagh, not least because they are noticeably more likely to go to school by public transport or by cycle. The focus groups showed how, in Helsinki, for many participants learning how to use the public transport system is part of their identity as accomplished urban citizens. It is the public transport system that gives them the consciousness that they can move about their city, that they have choices, and hence that in these terms, they can control their lives through the use of public structures. In

Helsinki, but unlike in Dublin, some older members of our focus groups linked public transport and public spiritedness. For them, part of the definition of public transport is that it is owned by 'the public' and good citizenship involves a preference for public means.

Mobility therefore means more than just moving from A to B. In the SceneSusTech study we termed such mobility 'target-oriented mobility' or *instrumental* mobility. Since such mobility is undertaken for a specific purpose, we can ask whether we can do it more quickly, or whether physical mobility is necessary in order to achieve the objective. By contrast, mobility also involves notions of exercising choice, of being in control, of getting around. We could term this mobility *expressive* mobility. Just like instrumental mobility, expressive mobility can be exercised through any mode of transport. In fact, much of the attraction of the car is the freedom of choice that it offers: we can stop at that café, drop in to see a friend, change plans easily etc. The majority of our interviewees from Athens and Dublin did indeed see the car in this way, and for them, as one remarked, "life without a car is meaningless". However, the focus groups in Bologna and Helsinki also showed that just walking or using public transport could be understood in the same way. In these cities the public transport system gave our respondents the consciousness that they could move about their city, that they had choices, and hence that they could use public facilities to control their own lives.

Public transport is called 'public' not because it is owned by the state or the municipality (this is in fact decreasingly the case), but because it is also partly itself a public space, since it is used by people *together*. It involves the commonality and passing companionship of fellow passengers rather than the individualised isolation of the 'carcooned' driver. The bus or the tram are 'public' in the same way that the pavement is: they can be used by many different sorts of people, all of whom are strangers to each other, and all of whom have to behave towards each other with some basic civility.

In the second half of the 20th century public transport has been denigrated in comparison to the attractions of the individual car. And travelling on an over-crowded DART or (even now) Luas can certainly make controlling one's own space within a car very attractive, even if the car is stuck in a traffic jam. It was therefore rather surprising that across the SceneSusTech study as a whole those who travelled to work by public transport were marginally more likely to enjoy their journey than those who travelled by private car. Partly this was simply because the alternative was worse: there was an almost complete consensus that 'The time is past when one could enjoy driving the car [in the city]' (focus group respondent, Helsinki). Nonetheless, in Bologna and Helsinki, some focus group participants described travelling by public transport as something they enjoy for its own sake. For older residents in Bologna the efficient bus service was a source of social contact. As one remarked: 'At our age, the more people you see the better.' For such respondents, public transport was pleasurable because it involved shared public space.

Safety in public places

The new urbanism is open to the charge of romanticising public spaces, ignoring how public spaces can become dangerous places. This blindness is part of a wider issue, the extent to which focus on the rights of citizenship has to be supplemented by the obligations of citizenship. If urban spaces are necessary for the rights of urban citizenship, the effective use of public space depends upon the exercise of the duties of citizenship. Ultimately, rights without duties are a denial of citizenship, because it places individuals in an exploitative relationship to the physical and social world that surrounds them. If I demand 'my rights' but refuse to do 'my duties', I am saying that society must contribute to me, but I have no obligation to it: in other words I am not actually part of it all. Such philosophical debates have practical consequences. Confronted by a world in which individuals do not exercise their obligations in public space, people flee to individual security – thus hastening the demise of public space. Effective public transport is interwoven with public safety, both in the streets and on the transport itself.

Safety in areas

For urban planners the city centre of Bologna is iconic, the first Italian city centre to be rescued from the motorcar. Bologna's covered arcades and the Piazza Maggiore are 'outdoor living rooms' for the citizens and the epitome of what the new urbanism wants to achieve. However, our research showed a gap between this image and the reality that has implications for Dublin.

In the SceneSusTech survey we measured the 'walking quality' of each area. We asked questions such as whether the traffic was intrusive and whether people felt safe from physical attack. To our surprise, the Centro Storico received one of the *lowest* scores of all twelve study areas. Particularly important here was the question of personal safety – in terms of which inner city Bologna was seen as one of the worst areas. Respondents were most likely to disagree with the statement 'I personally feel safe from attack' in the suburban working class areas of Dublin (60%) and Athens (55%), and in inner city Bologna (58%). There is growing anecdotal evidence that pedestrianisation of inner city areas attracts 'street people' whom the inhabitants find threatening – shortly after the survey was carried out, there was a much publicised murder in the Piazza Maggiore in the heart of Bologna's centro storico. By contrast, the lack of safety in working class Athens and Dublin areas shows a

destruction of public space by some inhabitants themselves; in particular young males make others unwilling to
use the streets.

There is of course often a disjunction between the fear of
crime and the actual level of crime. Furthermore, the fear of
crime can actually facilitate crime. Thus in the USA gated
communities are growing in areas that actually already have
relatively low levels of crime (Luymes, 1997), but by hunker-
ing down behind private security guards, their inhabitants
abandon public space which thus becomes more dangerous.
Equally, parents' fear that their children will not be safe to
walk or cycle to school is another self-fulfilling prophecy.
Children who are driven to school are less able to navigate
roads by themselves. Because there are fewer cyclists, car
drivers become even more careless of the remaining non-
motorised road users. However, public policy does have to
address these fears, rather than pretending they do not exist.
In Dublin (and in other cities and even small towns) there is
an increasing and realistic fear of unprovoked violence on the
streets in the evenings. If public transport is reduced, then it
is more difficult for people to use the streets, but if public
transport is to be used more, then the streets have to be safer.
In the first instance this means a strong police presence – on
the street, not hiding in cars.

Safety on transport

Public transport has to be a safe place, not a dangerous
place. All too often, public transport appears abandoned to
forces that threaten to deny ordinary users the right to use
this public space. Loutish and threatening behaviour, graffiti, littering, all indicate that the perpetrator exercises his or
her use of the facility *at the cost of others*. Such behaviour has
of course a simple consequence – other citizens abandon
the facility as soon as they can, usually for private transport.

Accordingly, one of the first steps in restoring the New York subway system was zero tolerance for graffiti:

> 'Our view was that the fact that graffiti could not be con-trolled was saying to the public, no one is in control; pro-ceed at your own peril. Crime was very high – though actually less on the subway than elsewhere – and so we decided to take graffiti on. The system was completely cov-ered with graffiti – 6,200 train carriages, 470 stations, the depots, the shops. It was a kind of leprosy.' Bob Kiley, ex-head of New York's Metropolitan Transportation Authority, quoted in Wolmar (2002: 166)

In Dublin this lesson has been learnt on the Luas, which has a zero-tolerance policy for graffiti. Once the graffiti writers get their hands on Luas, the public space will have started to shrink.

On some routes of Dublin Bus by contrast, transport is 'public' only in the sense of an unpleasant and dangerous space. As one respondent from Jobstown told us:

> I was going to town last week. It was 10 in the morning and nobody could use upstairs. A lot of boys had got off at the community centre before 10 and I suppose they had come out from town because the bus was after coming from town and whatever they were at, they had made a public toilet of upstairs (Nora).

Or again:

> One Sunday afternoon, I got on the bus, because I had the baby and the other little girl with me. Two young fellahs got on and a girl and they are from Jobstown...There was a man upstairs and he was listening to the way they were talking and he came down and he was drunk and he asked the bus-driver to stop the bus and to call the police because

he was so fed up with the way they were talking. Well, with that the bus-driver stopped the bus, shut the doors and called the police and no one could get on or off the bus. And the bus was packed and the three teenagers came down and they were shouting abuse at everybody...saying he is an auld drunk and ye listened to him... The police, of course are never around when you want them. So somebody broke the back door on the bus... She took herself and her daughter off the bus and I got off after her through the broken door and the bus was still sitting there an hour and a half afterwards (Joan).

Indeed at one stage in 2002 SIPTU members on Dublin Bus even went on strike because of what they had to endure driving certain routes in Tallaght. Incidents ranged from 'fights between passengers, to drivers being spat at, urinated on, assaulted and having their buses stoned' (Irish Times, 17.05.2002). Such destruction of public facilities by those who are meant to use them is not confined completely to the excluded working class suburbs of the city. In Dublin, 'middle class' public transport spaces can be undermined, for newspapers have also reported threatening behaviour on the DART. If public spaces are dangerous, the sensible person avoids them and gets into his (or in particular, her) car.

PUBLIC TRANSPORT AND THE PUBLIC REALM

One difference between Europe and the USA is the importance of what can be called the 'public domain' or the 'public realm':

'This social capability is supported by a conception of the public realm whose underwriting of public science, *public transport*, public art, public networks, public health, public broadcasting, public knowledge and the wider public interest gives European civilization its unique character while offering many of its enterprises competitive advantage.' (Hutton, 2002: 258-259, emphasis added).

The 'public realm' in this sense is a sphere of activity that is not defined by the market. It is, however, not a private or personal area, since it is one to which all citizens have access. It is a space where ultimately decisions are made by political rather than by market processes. Creating such a space has costs, but these are borne from general taxation and thus are paid by all citizens. This is justified because activities in the public realm, so it is argued, are important for the society as a whole. The public realm is not just about public costs, but also, and more importantly, about public usage. The public realm is used by 'the public', and in a way this very usage creates 'the public'. Usage of public facilities characterises people not just as individuals, but *also* as members and even as citizens of this society. The public in this sense is not just a collection of individuals; it is individuals who, even though they have no personal connection with each other, have some mutual connections and some real, if limited, mutual responsibility.

Such notions of the 'public' are not socialist, even though traditionally social democratic parties and (sometimes) trade unions have supported the collective provision of facilities. Indeed, some such public realm is essential in any democratic polity, however right wing or socially conservative. However, Hutton's argument is that the public realm is more developed in Europe, not least because European *conservative* politicians have traditionally understood private property as involving duties as well as rights. The European public realm is as much the creation of European christian democracy as of European social democracy. It puts forward a model of a democratic market society in which individuals are both private consumers and public citizens, and recognises that the quality of life requires that both elements are taken seriously. This particular mixture of welfare state and economic and social rights has been called the European Social Model (Wickham, 2002). This concern with the cohesion of society in many ways defines Europe (or at least 'old Europe') as different from the USA, where private property is seen as having absolute rights, where extremes of rich and poor are socially acceptable, and where high levels of violence are tolerated and even encouraged.

As Hutton's quote suggests, a strong public realm is not simply compatible with private enterprise, it can arguably provide firms with 'competitive advantage'. Such advantages range from a functioning physical infrastructure (e.g. good transport links), through an educated labour force to a culture of trust and mutual responsibility. The last is a clear example of 'social capability' or what is now often termed 'social capital'. Where people trust each other, where fraud and crime are low, then business spends less time and money enforcing contracts, guarding against theft, etc. However, for its advocates such purely *economic* advantages of a strong public realm are convenient, but beside the point. A strong public realm is desirable in itself; it is a moral or ethical demand, an inherent component of the good society.

Today the public realm is contested. On the one hand, many European politicians and indeed much of the European Commission promote economic 'reforms' such as labour market deregulation and the privatisation of state enterprises that risk undermining key components of the European Social Model. More locally, ideologues such as the Competition Authority promulgate a world in which only decisions made by individual consumers have any rationality or legitimacy. In Ireland the course of the Celtic Tiger showed a clear preference by politicians, and arguably in fact by most of the population, for private over public consumption[1]. On the other hand, there is a new and growing demand for areas of life shaped by public rather than market values. One obvious source is the 'anti-globalisation' movement, which remains far stronger on the European continent than in Ireland or Britain. However, the demand for the re-assertion of the public realm is not confined to such new social movements. Interestingly, and particularly post-Enron, some 'mainstream' economic commentators are realising that the American Business Model is not the only way to run a market economy, just as post-Iraq many European politicians have understood that Europe's interests are hardly served by an unquestioning acceptance of US foreign policy.

The city has a particular role in this debate. The public realm is not necessarily a physical place. For example, in Ireland most political debates occur in the media, including radio phone-ins and TV chat shows; local 'town hall' meetings are hardly important if they occur at all. Yet the city as a physical place is potentially an important component of the public realm. People who live in the same city, even if they do not live in the same neighbourhood, do share common physical places and common physical spaces. The city's shopping streets and public facilities are known to all. Thus the city has a shared physical reality that the nation often does not have. At the same time, the city is not 'an urban village' (though it may contain urban villages). The city is a space used by strangers who nonetheless have something in common. In this the city displays a key characteristic of a modern democracy: it is based not on links of family and kinship but on abstract social links (being Irish does not depend on knowing all Irish people).

At the same time, the physical reality of the city is part of people's lives in a way that the physical reality of the national territory is not. Here public transport is crucial, for it is public transport that literally ties the city together. Public transport increases the chances that all citizens can have access to the same spaces. Part of being a citizen of a city is the right to move around the city and to share this right with other citizens. This right is shared with visitors (and in this sense, the city is far more open and welcoming than the nation state, which reserves many of its welfare facilities for national citizens). Public transport therefore is part of the physical infrastructure of urban citizenship; it is one of the ways in which inhabitants become citizens. Strengthening Dublin's *public* transport system is one of the most important changes that can make Dublin a city with citizens rather than just inhabitants.

Note:
1. Yet again, this preference is based on the bad experience of Irish public services, leading to a self-fulfilling prophecy. Irish public services are under-funded, so they perform badly, so the public is unwilling to fund them.

Chapter 7

Is privatisation the solution?

Today Ireland has a new religion. For some people in government and in academe, let alone in private business, the ability of competition to produce improvement in every area of life is an article of faith. The state no longer gives the Roman Catholic church primacy over the affairs of the nation, but instead funds the 'Competition Authority'. Just as the Inquisition hunted down heresy, so the Competition Authority pursues 'anti-competitive behaviour' in every corner of economic life. Belief in competition is not, however, confined to such state-sponsored fanatics. For many people, confronted with the obvious failures of public transport in Dublin, one normal response is to call for 'more competition'. If only Dublin Bus workers – let alone Irish Rail managers – knew that they could lose their jobs if they did not provide a better service, then surely things would get better? At the same time, people are aware of the palpable failures of privatisation of public transport in the UK. Compared with ten or fifteen years ago, the problems of competition have also become more apparent.

In transport 'competition' and 'privatisation' take many different forms. Current government proposals are not to simply hand over public transport, or even Dublin buses, to the free market. Officially at least the government plans a *regulated* market to ensure that competition and private enterprise will deliver public services that will be superior to either the existing status quo or a pure market situation. Government plans were set out in several documents: 'A New Institutional and Regulatory Framework for Public Transport' (Department of Public Enterprise, 2000), the so-called 'Red Book'; a 'Consultation Paper' (the 'Blue Paper') entitled 'New Institutional Arrangements for Land Use and Transport in the Greater Dublin Area' (published jointly by the Department of the Environment and Local Government and the Department of Public Enterprise in March 2001).

The Red Book proposed the creation of a fully franchised bus market in the Greater Dublin Area and the eventual privatisation of Dublin Bus; it also proposed a new Railway Safety Authority and three separate entities responsible for the railway itself: an infrastructure company, an operating company, and an 'infrastructure procurement body'. The Blue Paper also proposed a 'strategic land use and transportation body' for the Greater Dublin Area that would be responsible for transport and land use planning and for regulating the Dublin bus market. Such plans appeared to have been completely abandoned, but then suddenly were resurrected at the end of 2005 when a new Dublin Transport Authority was announced as part of the government's 'Transport 21' investment plans. In the meantime the Railway Procurement Agency was set up and took over the building of Luas from CIÉ; the operation of Luas was franchised to Connex, a multi-national company. Trade union opposition has prevented the sale of Dublin Bus so far, but there are now more private bus operators in the Dublin area.

There is certainly more competition and private sector involvement in public transport in Dublin than in the past. The chapter begins by examining the conventional arguments for competition, particularly within a 'franchised' market. Franchising is not the same as simple deregulation, but as the second part of the chapter shows, it nonetheless has costs that are often ignored. The final part of the chapter suggests that competition can destroy any ethos of public service within public transport.

FROM FREE-FOR-ALL TO FRANCHISING

Regulating the market
Some notions of competition within public transport are wildly impractical. Thus in the 1980s the UK conservative government deregulated the local bus industry. The Minister of Transport, Nicholas Ridley, seriously believed that this would lead to a bus industry comprising a multitude of small independent operators:

> On Ridley's tours around the country [before deregulation], he was wont to ask local bus managers how many of their drivers owned their buses. Receiving the answer 'none', the minister would tell the hapless chap that he ought to consider the idea of selling off the buses to the drivers (Wolmar, 1999: 44).

The attempt to make operating local buses an example of pure competition as taught in first year economics text books ignores that in the bus industry, as in almost all industries, there are economies of scale and sheer size brings competitive advantages. The 1985 UK Transport Act both *privatised* the British bus industry, by breaking up and selling the National Bus Company, and also *deregulated* the market outside of London by allowing any company to set up routes with minimal restrictions. The role of the state became simply to licence companies to enter the market and regulate their behaviour (in terms of safety and some minimal standards). While local authorities were still allowed to subsidise public transport, they could only do so by putting loss-making routes out to competitive tender. This was enough to force municipally owned bus companies into private ownership. Although this did initially lead to a multitude of small operators, most were soon bought up or driven out of business as the industry became dominated by a few large operators, above all Stagecoach (Wolmar, 1999).

Many areas of public transport are a natural monopoly. On bus routes where passenger density is high, it is possible for two competing operators to survive. Even here, it is not clear that passengers will always benefit from this competition, since much competition is simply aimed at undermining the other operator. For example, just like competing railway companies in the 19th century, rival bus companies will not tell passengers about their rivals' timetable, so passengers will end up taking buses that are more inconvenient or more expensive than those actually on offer. On low-density routes, by contrast, it is usually only possible for one operator to survive. Here 'competition' just means that a private monopoly replaces a state-owned monopoly. Outside of London bus privatisation in the UK has been a failure. By 2002 fares had risen 87% in real terms since 1974, while motoring costs had remained constant. Passenger numbers are down, and integration between routes is weak, while integration with other transport modes (above all rail) is very poor (Joseph, 2002).

In the last few years some improvements *have* occurred, but these are more due to effective intervention by local authorities rather than because of initiatives by the private bus operators. The key role of local government is shown by London, which is also a good example of a franchise system. In London the state (through Transport for London) creates the market: it decides on routes and fares and then franchises the operation to private sector companies. Using this structure TfL has turned around bus use, with more and better-integrated routes. Bus ridership has been rising steadily since the early 1990s and has now regained the level of 1969 (TfL, 2003: 4).

On the railways of course the opportunities for competition between different railway companies are even less than on the buses. That is why historically railway companies developed as monopolies for geographical areas, and why competition between competing companies led to over-provision of under-used facilities (different railway stations in the same town, etc.). Nonetheless, the UK Conservative government of the 1990s was so obsessed by its own free enterprise ideology that it went even further than the 19th century. It determined to create competition between companies running trains over the same tracks! This required a horrendously complicated administrative structure. At the very simplest, there had to be separate companies responsible for the infrastructure (track, signalling, stations etc.) and operating (running the trains).

Safety on the railways had steadily improved under nationalised British Rail, but after privatisation there were fatal accidents at Southall in 1997 and Ladbroke Grove in 1999, both widely held to have been caused by the chaos of multiple companies running the railways. When a train came off the rails at Hatfield in October 2000 and four people died there was no longer any room for doubt: the crash was caused by faulty maintenance, itself the result of the system of subcontracting which had been imposed with privatisation. By then Britain's railways appeared to be in total collapse and 76% of the British electorate considered that the railways should be simply returned to public ownership (Murray, 2001: 168).

The Irish government would claim that it has learnt from the errors of privatisation in the UK. As far as the buses are concerned, the Red Book proposed a franchise system in which some or all bus routes are franchised to private operators on the basis of some form of competitive tendering. The government (through its regulatory agency) decides on the services, and then looks for the best company to operate them. Instead of competition 'in the market', as when private companies compete on the same routes, now there is competition 'for the market', with companies competing for routes.

For its advocates, franchising within a regulated market is seen as delivering the advantages of marketisation without the problems associated with a free for all. On the one hand, each route (or series of routes) is operated by a single operator, so the advantages of the single operator are retained (the natural monopoly argument). On the other hand, since franchises are awarded competitively and for a limited period, the advantages of competition are retained. Inefficient companies will not win franchises; companies that do not perform adequately will not get their franchises renewed. Furthermore, the system is transparent. Within a franchising system, it is relatively simple for the regulatory authority to allow local authorities to subsidise individual routes. Rather than giving a semi-commercial state organisation a subsidy over which the government has no control, the government (or local authority) uses a subsidy to 'buy' particular services from the transport company. Better still, since the franchise is not necessarily renewed, the government can ensure that it gets the best possible service for the citizens. Just as government contracts for the supply of toilet paper in government offices are awarded by competitive tender, so too now is the provision of public transport. Such an arrangement, so it could be claimed, allows clear political decisions to be made about the level of service that the state should provide for its citizens, and provides incentives to ensure that the citizens get the best deal.

Introducing such regulated competition on railways is necessarily more complex. Railways have expensive existing infrastructure (tracks, stations, etc.) and expensive rolling stock, which also has a long useful life. Furthermore, running a railway network is much more complex than running a bus network, not least for the simple reason that trains have to share tracks. And this in turn makes the question of safety more important and more complex than on the buses. Not for nothing were the railway companies of the 19th century the world's first large scale non-military bureaucracies.

In Ireland so far there has been no serious discussion of outright privatisation of Irish Rail. There seems to still be a belief that the state should retain control of the key assets, at very least the track and other infrastructure. Nonetheless, the Red Book did propose that the new railway operating company could be privatised, or that some or all railway services could be franchised. Irish Rail has been held in such low esteem that there was no opposition to cutting it out from any involvement in Luas. CIÉ's Light Rail Project Office was hived off into the separate Railway Procurement Agency, which then completed the construction of Luas. The RPA owns the track and rolling stock, while again without any opposition or even public discussion, the operation of Luas was franchised to Connex.

The arguments for competition

The most obvious argument for competition is that it forces operating companies to reduce their costs. In terms of bus transport it is clear that this is true. Since the mid-1980s all across the world urban bus markets have been opened to competition. Within the EU, apart from the UK, this has usually been through various forms of franchising. All reviews of the evidence show that competition, whether through franchising or through open markets, reduces costs (e.g. GommezIbanez and Meyer, 1997). For example, a review of transport in Dublin and nine other cities for the Public Transport Partnership Forum reported that costs were on average 25% lower within regulated markets compared to within closed markets (NERA and TIS.PT, 2001).

These gains will apply even if the company actually providing the service is nominally publicly owned. A state owned company will have to compete directly with private operators, and will tend to adopt similar practices.

Trade unions often argue that the only way private transport operators can cut costs is by cutting wages. Certainly, after deregulation in 1986 wage rates fell in the UK, even in London. According to one study, hourly wage rates fell 'by at least 16%' in London between 1987 and 1992 (Kennedy, 1995); according to Transport for London, bus driver wages 'fell in real terms by around 7-10% between 1986-98' (TfL, 2003: 24). Although Stagecoach, the largest bus operator in the UK, recognises unions, its wage rates are lower than the municipally owned companies it replaced (Wolmar, 1999). Clearly, private operators are able to use the threat of redundancy and competition to push down wage rates in ways that public enterprises are not able to do.

However, wage rates are only one aspect of overall wage costs. Companies operating in a competitive market (or competing for a market) usually control labour more closely than public enterprises (tighter control of absenteeism and sick leave) and also deploy labour more effectively. This partly involves challenging the 'restrictive practices' of unions, but it also involves simply more efficient management. Private operators have also cut costs by better engineering and maintenance, by making more use of cheaper suburban depots, and by cutting out management slack (Kennedy, 1995; also Wolmar, 1999). Unlike wage cuts, these savings are not necessarily at the cost of workers.

Large international operators such as Connex or Stagecoach are clearly able to bring new ideas into their local operations. Unlike CIÉ, Connex has experience of running tram systems in Europe and has brought these to the Luas. Stagecoach brought its experience of operating buses in the UK to its operations in Sweden. However, major improvements in bus services have occurred because of public initiative. Dublin's QBCs are now being taken as a model in other countries, and they owe virtually nothing to private sector initiative.

A final potential advantage of competition is access to capital. Public transport needs not just operating subsidies, but also investment. Especially in railways, such investment needs long term planning. Yet if the transport is state-controlled, then investment is normally on a 'stop-go' basis. As occurred in Ireland for decades, transport is starved of investment for long periods, especially if there is pressure to reduce government debt. Then suddenly politicians decide to pour investment into the system, and often cancel it again at short notice. Furthermore, politicians prefer grandiose new projects that are highly visible rather than more low-key routine investment necessary for maintaining the system. Part of the appeal of competition is that private sector involvement will allow easier and more predictable access to capital.

THE COMPLEXITIES AND COSTS OF REGULATION

When public transport is franchised, there has to be a contract between the state body controlling the market and the operating company. The role of the contract is to compel the operating company to provide as good a service as possible for as little subsidy as possible.

In theory the contract creates greater transparency, since it is clear what the state is purchasing and whether or not the operator is meeting its targets. Franchising requires monitoring different aspects of service provision (e.g. punctuality, cleanliness, timetabling information, driving standards etc) and this information can be in the public realm. Transport for London has the performance targets for each of its routes on its website. Here the contrast with Dublin Bus and Irish Rail is dramatic: despite 'partnership' and despite some real service improvements on Dublin Bus, neither company has any public monitoring of its service standards. However, it is important to notice that changing to a franchise model would not of itself guarantee transparency. For example, the general public cannot easily discover the performance targets that Connex has been set for the Luas.

More fundamentally, contracts have clear downsides, which stem from the nature of the relationship between the two parties. As a private company, the operator will be under pressure to produce profits for its shareholders, and in the age of shareholder value such profits are needed as soon as possible. At the same time, the state itself will try to ensure that the supplier remains exposed to the threat of competition and so will try to avoid long-term commitments. The relationship between the two sides is therefore potentially antagonistic.

Since neither side trusts the other very much, there is enormous pressure for ever-more details of the service to be formally specified in the contract. Precise penalties for inadequate performance have to be specified: how much does every late bus cost the operator? Performance has to be measured and monitored; it has to be agreed when the operator is not held responsible for failures (e.g. when there is increased traffic congestion on the bus route). As in all low trust relationships, this means that considerable expense, effort and expertise are required to monitor performance and attribute quantifiable costs and benefits. And because so much hangs on legal interpretation, the two sides can easily slide into a legal 'arms race'. When one side equips itself with a strong legal team, the other side has no alternative but to do the same. This is a mode of economic activity that generates large numbers of accountants and lawyers, since the costs of each activity have to be precisely measured and the two sides relate to each other only in terms of the contract.

Monitoring performance is central to the contract. Consequently, it is all too easy for performance to focus narrowly on targets rather than on the more general if not always precisely defined issue of providing a real public service. Equally, because performance becomes specified in detail by the contract, this itself makes it difficult for the operator or the authority to innovate during the lifetime of the contract.

If the policy objective is to increase competition between companies, this will lead to a multiplicity of operators and even more complicated contractual relationships. Thus the privatisation of British Rail with its division between the infrastructure and the operating companies means that when delays occur, the operator and the infrastructure company dispute the cause of the delay. Rather than expending effort improving the system, companies employ staff to shift the blame onto another company: 'fault attribution has become an industry in its own right' (Wolmar, 2001: 197). These contractual and often competitive relationships destroy any expertise about the system as a whole, and undermine employees' and managers' competence and commitment. This has particular consequences for safety:

> 'A single organisation, the railway, cannot be satisfactorily run exclusively by legal contractual relations. Tightly specified contracts are incapable of creating co-operative commitment to safety: no contract can ever eliminate the space for parties not to pursue its terms wholeheartedly.'
>
> John Hendy QC, leading counsel for the bereaved and injured at the Ladbroke Grove and Southall inquiries (as quoted in Wolmar, 2001: 255).

The proposal to franchise Dublin bus routes is not the same as the complete deregulation imposed on the local bus industry in the UK outside of London. It is also relatively simple compared with the multitude of operators and agencies involved in British railways, or even the horrendous and possibly unworkable complexities of 'Public Private Partnership' imposed by the UK government on the London Underground. The problems in the proposal are real enough but they should not be confused with these rather different systems.

A franchising system is no 'magic bullet' for public transport. It would probably reduce operating costs, but Dublin Bus is now already a relatively cost-efficient operator. It certainly would not entirely eliminate the need for public subsidy. Discussion of competition pushes the debate towards a focus on costs, whereas the key question should be whether public transport as a whole contributes to reducing car dependency. What matters above all is simply whether use of public transport is increasing. There is not much point in having a cost-efficient system that just comprises a few residual routes. Once the question is posed like this, one realises that much of the rhetoric about 'innovation' is also beside the point. Major improvements in public transport depend very largely on public decisions and cooperation between transport companies and public authorities. One obvious example – Dublin's QBCs have contributed to a revival of bus use in Dublin, but this has had almost nothing to do with 'private sector dynamism'.

EROSION OF PUBLIC SERVICE ETHOS

From the standpoint of economic theory and of competition policy, in the private sector companies only work for profits, employees only work for wages. In the real world neither statement (but particularly the second one) is completely true. Such often absurd simplifications do, however, have a political message: to the extent that the public sector is different from the private sector, then that simply proves that it is worse. Accordingly, public sector organisations should either be privatised or, if that is impossible, made to become as similar as possible to the private sector. As we shall now see, this ignores that public enterprises are part of the common public sphere, they exist to serve citizens not customers and they can therefore command a different form of loyalty from their employees. Paradoxically, any real reform of public transport organisations would actually accentuate these differences.

State enterprises

It is frequently argued that public enterprises should become more 'commercial', 'entrepreneurial' or 'market oriented'. While this may appear to be self-evidently desirable, it is actually rather problematic.

A key characteristic of a state enterprise is that, even if it is profitable overall, it carries out activities that are not commercially justified. These tasks and their rationale can vary enormously: taking on extra employees in order to reduce unemployment, training apprentices in order to counter-act a national skill shortage, installing filtration systems to protect the environment, even installing telecommunication links to facilitate multi-national companies[1]. In the case of public transport, the key issue is of course the provision of services that do not cover their own costs. The argument of the 'New Public Management' is that such activities should be clearly identified so that the state can then explicitly pay for them. This should allow more rational decision-making. Once the cost of such subsidies is identified, then it becomes in principle possible to decide between different and competing uses of public funds. Paradoxically, such accounting techniques become an argument for privatisation, since if the 'public service' element of a state company's activities is identified and charged separately, then there is no reason for the enterprise as a whole to be state-owed.

However, if private companies are going to provide public services, this creates its own problems. If the private company is a monopoly, then a private monopoly has simply replaced a public monopoly and this creates the need for extensive regulation. Equally, if there is competition between enterprises providing the service (as in a deregulated bus market), then the fragmentation of service will not necessarily benefit the consumer. As we have seen, franchising and other forms of market-based regulation often require complex and rigid contracts to ensure that the service is actually delivered.

Such forms of governance run the risk of creating 'perverse incentives'. If performance is measured (and profits affected) by tightly defined standards, then this will focus the attention of the company – and of its employees – on meeting precisely those standards. The letter of the contract will be followed, rather than the spirit. The emphasis is on making profits (or minimising penalties) rather than fulfilling the overall service itself. In particular, co-operation with other companies can be penalised rather than rewarded. Thus in the UK several new light rail systems have not met their financial targets (National Audit Office, 2004). One reason is that competition policy actually makes co-ordination between transport companies 'anti-competitive' (see also Joseph, 2002).

Safety on the privatised British rail system is a notorious example of this problem. On the nationalised system, staff would report safety incidents as part of a general (if vaguely defined) sense of professional duty, but once they became focused on immediate performance targets there was little incentive for them to report safety incidents 'especially as staff do not have the same public sector ethos as they were imbued with at BR' (Wolmar, 1999: 184). Measuring all elements of performance in order to identify the specific public service elements therefore undermines the general public service ethos of the enterprise.

Conversely, the public service ethos is *potentially* part of the general 'culture' of a public enterprise. It becomes part of what the enterprise 'is': isolating and costing its distinct elements runs the risk of destroying it.

In many European countries, public utilities are seen as public enterprises, not least because they provide services considered essential for all citizens. Thus the French concept of 'service publique' makes clear that state enterprises belong to the people and serve the people. As John Kay points out, this means to say that we, the citizens, do actually consider them 'ours' in the way that we do not see private companies (Kay, 2002). For Dubliners, Dublin Bus is not Burger King, nor even Aircoach. At its best, public enterprise can therefore call on the support of citizens in a very different way from the 'brand loyalty' of consumers. Dublin Bus's new slogan 'Serving the Whole Community' appeals to this form of loyalty.

There is an important issue here for public transport. People increasingly recognise the environmental damage caused by car usage. People are probably more likely to heed appeals to use public transport if they are not simply contributing to a private company's profits. In the SceneSusTech focus groups in Bologna and Helsinki, some participants explicitly linked public transport with public spiritedness. Similarly, a recent study of transport users in French and Swiss cities identified a small minority of 'civic ecologists' who used public transport for primarily ideological reasons 'out of respect for the environment' (Kaufmann, 2002: 69). A private enterprise has a legal obligation to prioritise the interests of its shareholders, but this makes it more difficult for it to appeal for customers in terms of the public good!

Privatisation by definition means selling public assets. Whatever the short-term gains for governments may be, the disposal of public assets not only reduces the resources at the state's disposal, but replacing them is often prohibitively expensive. In the public transport area the negative consequences can now surface quickly. Thus in the UK, the Strategic Rail Authority found that it could not re-install railway lines in line with new passenger demand, because Railtrack, attempting to maximise the value of its assets, had sold off much 'surplus' land[2]. There are obvious lessons here for the government's current plans to use CIÉ's land bank to fund privatisation (above all to 'buy out' employees).

Privatisation also narrows the area of life in which actions can only be justified if they contribute to the 'bottom line'. One simple example – the Freedom of Information Act compels public authorities to provide information to citizens on request. However, to the extent that services are provided by private companies, increasingly information is withheld as 'commercially sensitive'. Whereas a public enterprise will often provide information from a general sense of public duty, private enterprises are likely to reduce the information available to the public because there is no commercial case for providing it. According to some researchers, research on public transport provision is becomingly more difficult for this very reason[3].

Citizens and customers

When a private company provides a service to a customer, it does so because the customer is paying for it. Rights to the service are conditional on paying for it. Equally, the firm only offers the service if it can be expected to be profitable. In many countries private sector banks are withdrawing facilities from low-income customers and low-income areas, for the simple reason that these are not profitable (Webster et al, 2002). 'The customer is always right' but only if the customer can afford the service.

Citizens, however, are different from customers, for citizens have rights irrespective of their income. If public transport is defined as a public service, then although there may be a charge for the service, there is also an element of citizenship *entitlement*, just as in European welfare states (but not the USA) citizens have entitlements to health, education and housing. From this perspective, within the public sector citizens are treated equitably, irrespective of their financial resources. Consequently the relationship between the employee providing the service and the citizen receiving the service is different.

Clearly the relationship between public sector employee and the public varies between services and between countries. Partly this depends on the occupation: it would be difficult to imagine that bus drivers would ever have the same commitment to their passengers as we routinely expect nurses to have to their patients. Equally it depends on the country: where citizen participation in state decision-making is high, then public employees are more likely to be committed to the welfare of their citizens than where the state is distant or even authoritarian. Irish political culture, with its clientelism and populism, is notoriously inhospitable to any idea of public service.[4] Nonetheless, public ownership provides the possibility for the development of public service in a way that private ownership does not.

In fact the failure of public enterprise to provide good customer service has been a key argument in favour of privatisation. Organisations such as Dublin Bus, let alone Irish Rail, have in the past been notorious for the customer-hostility of many frontline staff. Yet the relationship between private ownership and customer orientation is not clear-cut. On the one hand, given clear management and human resource policies, nationalised industries can develop a good customer-orientation. Examples include British Rail in its final decade before privatisation (Wolmar, 2001), perhaps also Aer Lingus and even incipiently Dublin Bus. On the other hand, while improved customer service was seen as one of the perceived benefits of privatising British Rail, it does seem that British train operators have failed to develop a customer service ethos:

> While a few train operators have developed a reputation for good customer care, most have barely matched BR's standards. Indeed, one of the most amazing failings of privatisation has been that the oft-repeated promises that the private sector would treat its customers much better than BR have been largely unfulfilled. In an assessment of customer service after privatisation Roger Ford, the highly regarded rail journalist, attempted to set out all the 'soft' improvements of service to passengers[5]. It proved to be a short list and indeed, some of the customer-friendly innovations made by BR had been scrapped (Wolmar, 1999: 195).

And in a warning note to those who expect better service if Dublin Bus were privatised:

> Ford attributes the paucity of initiatives on customer care to the fact that most of the franchisees are bus companies who have, traditionally, paid little regard to the needs of their passengers (Wolmar, 1999: 196).

Given tight cost accounting and above all, the attempt by operators to reduce staff costs, the idea that privatisation will produce better service to citizens seems naïve.

Public sector employment

For many ideologues, it is often axiomatic that the public sector is over-staffed. Indeed, one rationale of the 'New Public Management' is the assumption that public enterprises are run for the benefit of their own employees rather than for that of the public. In fact, much discussion of public sector employment ignores the fundamental differences between the public and the private sectors.

Most fundamentally, working involves some notion of 'equity': the state – and hence its employees – has to treat citizens in particular ways. This in turn means that work often involves some commitment to providing the actual service. For example, in a recent study of four Dublin workplaces, employees at Dublin Bus were particularly likely to be 'proud to work for this organisation' and usually explained this, as one put it, in terms of providing 'a public service, you know, not just public transport' (quoted in Doherty, 2006).

The greater this specific commitment, the clearer the *public service* quality of the employment. Although issues of pay and conditions are of course important to morale in the public service, it remains the fact that people often work in the public service in part because of commitment to the service they provide.

In fact this is particularly true of public sector management. There is growing evidence that, at least in some countries, public sector management is motivated differently to private sector management. Public sector managers do tend to value job security more highly than their private sector colleagues. However, one reason for this may well be that their skills and expertise are based on the particular area where they work. In other words, they value job security because their skills are less 'transferable' to other employers. More importantly, people often enter public service management with the belief that they are 'Not just making money' but 'Doing something that matters' (Brown and Scase, 1994). Again this involves a commitment both to the general idea of public service and to a specific area of work. The contrast to current fashions in the private sector could not be greater. Here increasingly it is assumed that managers can only be motivated by money, and that 'management' is a general skill that can be applied to any area of activity. Within this model, managers need know nothing about the particular industry in which they manage, and in particular need no experience of or commitment to what 'their' enterprises actually do.

The public sector has also traditionally been a key provider of good quality *low* skill jobs (Crouch et al, 2001: 239). This is a problem for opponents of the public sector. It shows that trade union power and/or political expediency has enforced conditions that cannot be justified in terms of the market. Without such protection, low skill workers in the public sector would have lower pay, worse conditions, less job security – the same conditions as those with similar qualifications in the private sector. However, this 'privileged' position of public sector workers can be justified. Ultimately, the state employs people to provide services because part of the role of the state is to maintain the *social cohesion* of the society. In this context, state services should be provided to citizens by fellow citizens who have some basic commitment to the work they are doing. Such commitment is unlikely to be forthcoming if state workers are treated as casual labour. From this perspective, higher earnings differentials within the public sector ('market rates' for public sector managers) should also be regarded as problematic, because they may demotivate public sector employees as a whole.

This suggests that job security in the public sector is not simply a trade-off for low pay, but can help ensure a proper public service to the public. Of course, Dublin's publicly owned transport organisations are living proof that job security by itself is no guarantee of anything. Disgracefully, on Irish Rail, union opposition to new working practices is already holding up new services. Clearly, the inner workings of these public companies need to be opened to public scrutiny; clearly there needs to be open monitoring of their performance right down to the level of the individual bus route or railway service. Here new bench marking techniques (such as the public display of punctuality levels or even absenteeism rates) are an obvious way forward.

Conventional public sector trade unionists would probably not be exactly enamoured of such transparency, but would find it impossible to resist if the issue was posed in terms of genuine public sector partnership. The problem today is that instead of using the partnership process to make public transport – and public transport unions – accountable to the public, it has been all too often used to facilitate the government's agenda of privatisation. Instead of developing a public sector ethos that would make sense for today's public transport, government policy undermines any possible basis for it.

CONCLUSION

Competition and privatisation are presented as ways of making public transport more efficient. This ignores that public enterprises can be reformed and can be made accountable. At worst, the call for 'efficiency' is simply a narrow focus on labour costs; even at best, it usually ignores the wider objectives which public transport increasingly has to serve. Public transport is now essential for sustainability, for social inclusion and even for maintaining urban public life. If public transport is to contribute to these objectives, then it is by no means clear that competition, even in the form of franchising and 'competition for the market', is necessarily the best solution. As the next chapter shows, what is clear is that effective urban public transport requires effective local government and effective governance. Fetishising 'competition' distracts from the more important institutional changes that are needed in Dublin.

Notes:
1   It is ironic that one cause of the 'Celtic Tiger' boom was the state's decision to dramatically upgrade the telephone system in

the 1980s. As the slow development of broadband in Ireland shows, such an investment would be impossible today with a privatised telecommunications system governed by a regulator who has to enforce competition!

2 One reason for the initial success of Railtrack privatisation was that investors expected it to make money from its property port-folio (Wolmar, 1999: 20)

3 Professor Jeff Kenworthy, personal communication.

4 The new Irish state developed an enviable reputation for honest (if penny-pinching) administration. This asset has now been squandered: one international survey reports Ireland is now seen as one of the most corrupt states in Europe.

5 The source is cited as Roger Ford, 'Customer Service', Modern Railways, November 1999.

Chapter 8

Putting Dublin back on track?
Governance and the city

C urrently the Irish government, or at least the Minister for Transport, is determined to tackle Dublin's traffic mess. Paradoxically, that itself is part of the problem. The single most important message from comparative research is that effective urban public transport depends on effective *city* government, and not the privatisation and marketisation that has dominated government concerns, at least until very recently.

What explains why some cities have more successful public transport than others? What are the common features of the (relative) success stories, and conversely, do the disaster zones like Athens and Dublin have things in common? The first part of this chapter shows that there is one clear lesson from such comparisons: the importance of a single 'Transit Authority' in charge of all modes of transport in a large city. Since Dublin is now to get such a Dublin Transport Authority, maybe the tide is about to turn? Unfortunately, it seems that what the politicians give with one hand, they take away with the other: the new DTA runs the risk of being yet another self-important body that actually achieves very little. As the second part of the chapter shows, the DTA will have to deal with a weak city government and completely ineffective regional or metropolitan structures. Furthermore, the third part of the chapter documents how Dublin has an undeveloped civic culture in which public engagement with the transport issue is at best sporadic and unstructured. As the final part of the chapter shows, the influence of the EU is very ambiguous. It has created pressure for better urban government, it has provided conduits through which European cities can learn from each other, but the EU is also increasingly a vehicle for privatisation policies which threaten to undermine the basis of any public transport system that actually serves the public.

A SINGLE PASSENGER AUTHORITY?

Comparing cities: the need for a single authority

As tourists all of us can notice how the quality of public transport varies between cities. There is now an increasing number of studies which ask why some cities do better than others.

In the course of the controversy over privatisation of Dublin Bus, the Public Transport Passenger Forum commissioned a study that compared Dublin with cities such as Adelaide, Copenhagen, Evora, Lyon, Manchester, Preston, The Hague, Toronto and Zurich. The study was narrowly defined as an evaluation of the funding arrangements for public transport provision in these cities. It compared three different models: a controlled state market with a single supplier (effectively the Dublin situation); a regulated market with routes or areas franchised through competitive tendering (as currently practised in London and as proposed for Dublin); and deregulated competition (as in most British provincial cities).

This report argued that while there was no one clear

best practice, Dublin was at a particular disadvantage
because it lacked a single passenger transit authority:

> Dublin is rather different from the other cities we have
> studied because no overall public transport authority exists
> apart from the Dublin Transportation Office established in
> 1995 with limited powers... The lessons from our case
> studies indicate the existence of a powerful public trans-
> port authority is highly beneficial. Most public authorities
> have achieved integrated networks, tariff integration and
> an overall co-ordination of the (public) transport system.
> (NERA and TIS.PT 2001: 226)

It is quite clear that an integrated network is the basis of
any effective public transport provision. This makes it
somewhat bizarre that Irish public policy has prioritised the
much more debatable objective of achieving 'competition'
in public transport.

A broader overview of the overall effectiveness of transport policy is provided by a study by Apel and Pharaoh
(1995). They compared ten European cities including Basel,
Bologna, Freiburg, London, Stockholm and Zurich.
Although all had had some success in restraining the
growth in car usage[1], only Basel, Freiburg and Zurich had
stabilised car ownership and usage within the city area.
Apel and Pharaoh argue that the most important policy
measures were an integrated transport system in which on-
street light rail usually played a key role. A necessary (but
not sufficient) condition for achieving this was an effective
and democratic local government that involved the citizens
in decision-making.

Whereas other studies have focused on successful cities,
the SceneSusTech project contrasted two 'worst practice'
cities (Athens and Dublin) with two best practice cities
(Bologna, Helsinki). This contrast allows some clear conclusions.

Bologna and Helsinki are clear cases of strong *local* government. Both cities have decision-making powers and some financial autonomy. Financial autonomy, which has to mean tax-raising powers, is essential if local autonomy is to have any meaning and local politicians to have any power – and accountability[2].

Helsinki is the capital city of Finland and its architecture and urban environment are important to Finnish national pride. However, national government plays a limited role in shaping the city. Both Helsinki and Bologna are also anchored in an effective regional or metropolitan level government structure. This allows transport planning to encompass the city's immediate hinterland and in the case of Helsinki in particular allows the transport planning to be linked to land use planning.

The contrast with Athens and Dublin is dramatic. In both cities the national government takes all major infrastructural decisions. In neither city is there an effective regional or metropolitan authority, so any coherent transport policy is impossible. National government may from time to time sanction major infrastructural projects (e.g. the Athens metro) but these do not provide an integrated system. While such prestige projects are sometimes popular with politicians, they can often detract from the less glamorous but equally important (and equally expensive) task of maintaining the existing networks (Wolmar, 2002: 38). Significantly, Apel and Pharaoh also notice that the achievements of London and Stockholm have been hampered by weak *national* policies, in particular the construction of urban ring roads that have led to car-based developments and so generated additional local motor traffic.

The importance of co-ordination is also shown by research on the success of city and regional public transport associations (Verkehrsverbünde) in the German speaking countries. A Verkehrsverbund brings together transport providers in a region to develop an integrated transport system, ranging from co-ordinating timetables to integrated ticketing. In fact, one of the most important ways that these associations have been able to increase public transport use is simply by creating monthly or even annual transport passes valid for any travel within the area (Pucher and Kurth, 1996) – something that eluded Dublin for years. Given that all Dublin transport has, until recently, been state owned, it is astonishing that no similar development ever occurred in the city.

From Dublin Transport Authority to...Dublin Transport Authority?

Just how seriously co-ordination of public transport was taken by national politicians is shown by the brief life of the first Dublin Transport Authority. Set up by the Fine Gael – Labour coalition government in 1986, it was abolished by the incoming Fianna Fáil government in 1987 (McDonald, 2000: 134). This decision ensured that Dublin's transport crisis accelerated as the slump of the 1980s turned into the boom of the late 1990s.

One response to the crisis had been the Dublin Transportation Initiative. Starting as yet another official review, this turned into a coalition of interest groups determined to tackle the transport crisis. Its flagship project was the idea of a light rail along the old Harcourt Street line and by 1991 Fianna Fáil included light rail for Dublin in its local elections manifesto (McDonald, 2000: 137). However, the proposal took so long to get off the ground that the coalition began to fall apart. The DTI morphed into the Dublin Transport Office which became another state sponsored lobby group, increasingly eschewing publicity and focusing on the technical issues of traffic management and traffic modelling. Although the DTO produced a comprehensive transport plan for Dublin – *Platform for Change* – this never had any official status and ten years after the abolition of the

DTA, there was still nobody in charge of Dublin transport.

The government's consultation paper 'New Institutional Arrangements for Land Use and Public Transport' proposed a 'Strategic Land Use and Transportation Body' for the Greater Dublin Area. As the name implies, this was to oversee both land use and transport in the GDA. The paper identified successful cities as having amongst other things:

> Strong, well resourced city government with responsibility for a wide range of functions, significant source of revenue and the capacity to effectively integrate various policies (Department of the Environment, 2001: 11).

Yet the consultation paper's proposed body was rather different. It was planned to incorporate the DTO but now with wide-ranging powers, but had no democratic mandate whatsoever (it was to be a quango of local councillors, social partners and government nominees, responsible only to the *national* government). All these documents accepted the privatisation of Dublin Bus and indeed the involvement of the private sector in the construction and running of public transport generally. In fact the government, and in particular the Department of Finance, remained determined to ensure that the existing semi-state companies should not benefit from any expansion of public transport. Accordingly, Luas – when it was finally built – was the first project of the new Railway Procurement Agency (RPA) and was operated by a franchise rather than by the state.

In 2005 the government announced its *Transport 21* plan for transport investment. Commentators claimed that many of the projects in the plan had already been announced. As far as Dublin public transport is concerned, this was not actually the case. Most of the projects in the plan had been suggested before, but the government had never made any commitment to anything beyond the extension of the Luas Red Line to the docklands. Some items were new, such as the plan for a central interchange at St. Stephen's Green. Almost unnoticed, the plans were actually *less* extensive than those put forward in the DTO's *Platform for Change* grand plan of 2000, even though it was widely accepted that the city's growth had already surpassed the DTO's projections – so logically, *Platform for Change* should have been lengthened, not trimmed.

Central to *Transport 21* was the promised creation of a new Dublin Transport Authority, but despite its title, this appeared to be conceived as responsible merely for ensuring the delivery of the new rail-based projects in the city on time and on budget. The worry is that the new DTA could turn out to be another device to avoid tackling the institutional spaghetti within which Dublin's transport is mismanaged.

LOCAL NON-GOVERNMENT

Dublin local government is notorious for its plethora of institutions, and this is especially the case in the transport area. Some of this complexity is normal and even inevitable. It is normal that in metropolitan city regions like Dublin the population outgrows the original boundaries; transport is particularly complex because it involves different modes (road, rail etc...), private and public actors, and crosses territorial boundaries. Furthermore, in recent years 'partnership' has become a value in Irish politics: it is assumed that in making decisions governments should try to include all 'stakeholders' and create consensus. The problem in Dublin is not complexity or even inclusiveness by itself. The problem is that Dublin's complexity and inclusiveness is dysfunctional.

Since at least the 1970s commentators have stressed the weakness of Irish local government in general. After electoral reform in 1840, Dublin Corporation became a constant irritant to the British authorities. Yet in 1923 the Local Government (Temporary Provisions) Act gave the new state's government power to simply suspend local authorities, something that no British Administration would have dared to do. In 1978 Irish local authorities lost any income from domestic rates and so became largely financially dependent on central government.

Local government in Dublin itself is also fragmented into four local authorities: Dublin City Council (the previous Dublin Corporation) and the three local authorities carved out of the old Dublin County Council: Fingal, Dun Laoghaire-Rathdown and South Dublin. Typically, although there have been proposals to create a regional authority for the Dublin area since the 1920s, these new Councils set up in 1985 are all autonomous.

Since the 1920s it has been recognised that there needs to be some overarching regional local authority for the greater Dublin area. The Dublin Regional Authority was created in 1991 under the Regional Government Act. It brings together the four Dublin councils, but has no effective powers. Although cynics refer to it as a device for increasing councillors' attendance expenses, it is beginning to serve a function as a meeting place for Dublin area councillors and there are even signs of the beginning of strategy at this level. For example, in 2005 quite fortuitously the Labour Party held the honorary mayoralty in all four authorities and held a 'four mayors' conferences to discuss issues at Dublin level amongst its members in Liberty Hall.

The combined population of the three surrounding counties of Kildare, Meath and Wicklow now approaches that of Dublin City; the total population of what is now effectively the Dublin metropolitan region is over 1.5 million. This 'Greater Dublin Area' is the area covered by the Dublin Transportation Office; this is also the area which, it was suggested, should be covered by the government's (now abandoned) proposed transport and land use planning authority. Yet there is not a single publicly elected or accountable body that covers this area. Probably the winner of the prize for the most meaningless public body goes, however, to the Southern and Eastern Regional Assembly. This was set up because, in order to obtain EU structural funds, the entire Republic was divided into a Border, Midlands and Western Region, which was designed as an 'Objective 2 Region' and so eligible for regional funds, and the rest of the country, which did not include such areas. This wonderful Assembly meets to discuss the affairs of a 'region' that includes the metropolitan region of Dublin and...the county of Kerry.

In this context local councillors have hardly any impact on transport policy. Since the 1990s local authorities have been required to set up Strategic Policy Committees but these seem to have had little impact on policy formulation. Within Dublin City policy depends effectively on the local officials and over the last ten years there has been a sea change in the outlook and policies of Dublin City officials. While he was the City's Director of Traffic, Owen Keegan pushed through policies to control parking and restrict traffic in the inner city area. As chief planner, John Fitzgerald, now city manager, was responsible for the Integrated Area Plans for the inner city that restricted cars through traffic cells. Such new officials have contacts with other city administrations across Europe, and one thing that defines them is their understanding of Dublin as a European city and their mutual learning of urban traffic management and urban planning. By contrast, officials in the other three Dublin authorities appear less 'plugged in' to international circuits; in the three suburban Dublin authorities, the power of developers is stronger and the authorities have been largely unable to harness private property interests for the common good. In such areas 'traffic' still means new roads largely and thus even more unsustainable forms of development.

Part of the problem is that local authorities have power to do a lot of damage, but relatively little power to make positive changes. Thus councils can promote roads, as we saw in Dublin in the 1980s when areas of inner Dublin were demolished for the notorious Inner Tangent road, and thus make room for more cars, but they cannot create more public transport. They have effectively no powers in relation to public transport and they certainly cannot initiate public transport infrastructure projects. Funds for projects such as Luas come entirely from central government.

In the city of Dublin local government is weak and there is no meaningful metropolitan or regional government at all. All major investment decisions for public transport are taken entirely by central government with virtually no input from local government. Indeed, when new areas of investment arise, they are handled by new national institutions reporting to central government. In the transport area, as in other areas of policy such as urban regeneration, agencies that operate locally are subordinated not to local government but to a department of national government and policy remains determined at national level. For example, the decision to finally build the two Luas lines was taken by national government, which even decided on the routes they should follow. The decision was implemented by the new Railway Procurement Agency (RPA), which again reported to the Department of Transport. The Dublin Transportation Office, the only body with serious expertise in the area, played a minimal role.

The story of transport can be repeated across other policy areas. In urban regeneration, initiatives such as Temple Bar and the Docklands Development Authority were explicitly designed to ensure that they by-passed local government. Dublin may be the intellectual powerhouse of the country and the centre of its 'knowledge-economy' but there is nothing that resembles any city or metropolitan higher-level educational policy – local authorities merely distribute student maintenance grants[3]. Such different areas all show the same symptoms: the lack of any clear overarching policy, a plethora of institutions and the attempt to involve as many actors as possible in decision-making.

Especially in the transport area, these features prevent decisions being made. When a problem arises it is not tackled. Instead, an institution is created to which the problem can be delegated – and then ignored. This is exacerbated by the stress on 'inclusion', because this creates the need for more public bodies onto which advocates of change can be promoted. Secondly, when things have to be done they are done by national agencies reporting not to the locally elected politicians but to national government, thus ensuring that local government is further weakened. Thus EU regional funds, which were intended to strengthen subnational governments, end up being administered by agencies reporting to... the Department of the Taoiseach. As one recent study remarked:

> [The] Dublin area now has one of the most convoluted structures of governance in the entire EU, a status which may ultimately threaten to undo its newfound success' (Marshall, 2002).

This institutional blockage is interwoven with two other issues that are less discussed. Firstly, the plethora of ineffective agencies ends up ensuring that many changes occur entirely outside the remit of the political system altogether, so a kind of 'Wild West' anarchic development sits *alongside* the extensive government agencies. The problem is *not* that there is no government, but that government is, so to speak, looking in the wrong place. Secondly, ineffective local government 'teaches' local citizens that government is ineffective and that there is no point in attempting to achieve change through the political system. The citizenry remains powerless and cynical.

The weakness of Dublin city government means that nobody within the city is responsible for the transport in the city. Nobody can be blamed, but equally nobody can be praised. The contrast with some European cities is remarkable. One aspect of Europe's urban renaissance since the 1980s has been the role of powerful local urban leaders who have built their career on successfully reviving their city: Pasqual Maragall in Barcelona, Pierre Mauroy in Lille, even Ken Livingstone in London. Crucial to this has been transport – and the success works both ways. The success of the new tramway in Strasbourg was also a success for the career of the mayor, Catherine Trautmann. The contrast with Ireland is instructive. Irish politicians do often start their careers at local level, but not a single Irish politician built a reputation on what they achieved for their city. In local politics, politicians learn the skills of clientelism, which they then transpose into national politics. In this situation, it is not surprising that Dublin's transport is at best a plaything for national politicians.

THE TRANSPORT ARENA AND ITS ACTORS

The crisis of the 1980s in Dublin led to the Dublin Transportation Initiative, a grouping which emerged not from the political parties, but from a collection of concerned individuals, city centre businesses and a new generation of city officials. This urban coalition generated for the first time a vision of Dublin as a capital city.

Quite rightly, Frank MacDonald's own account of the rebirth of Dublin gives a key role to the decision by Frank Feely, the then Dublin City Manager, to celebrate (however spurious the chronology) Dublin's 1,000th birthday in 1988. This was the point at which Dublin City officials changed from being villains to heroes. A new generation of officials were reaching positions of power who were aware of international discussions in urban policy and who shared a commitment to the reinvigoration of the inner city along what were increasingly defined as 'European' lines. Traffic planning was now about pedestrianisation, not about building urban motorways. These new officials were a crucial part of the new urban coalition, in which no city councillor played any significant role at all.

However, the origins of this alliance lie in the 1960s. In Dublin, as elsewhere in the world, 1968 was the year of student revolution. Rather unusually, in Dublin architectural students played a key role. The immediate cause of their revolt – which included a weeklong teach-in in Earlsfort Terrace – was the refusal of UCD to change the curriculum to prevent a de-recognition of the Irish qualification by the British profession[4]. However, architectural students had also been involved in the first political opposition to the demolition of Georgian Dublin, when they organised a sit-in to prevent the demolition of a Georgian building in St. Stephen's Green.

From this beginning through the 1970s a small and diverse group of activists began to campaign for a new approach to the city's physical development. Dublin now had, for almost the first time, its own urban intelligentsia. The 'Living City' group around the writer Deirdre Kelly campaigned for preservation of the city's built heritage; journalist Frank MacDonald began a long career as an environmental campaigner. This was certainly a new voice in the politics of the city, but it remained marginal. Even if one leader of the Earlsfort Terrace sit-in, Ruairí Quinn, went on to be the leader of the Labour Party, there were few links of any importance to party politics at city or at national level; Dublin city councillors continued to supervise the destruction of the city. The initial weakness of the movement is clear in international comparison: around this time in cities such as Helsinki and Bologna similar movements were strong enough to force a radical re-orientation of their cities' transport away from the car-based plans of the authorities. In Dublin, however, plans to expand the road system continued, and were stymied by a mixture of bureaucratic ineffectiveness and economic recession rather than public opposition and debate.

In the 1980s these individuals began to make links with the city centre business community, and here transport was crucial. Simon Perry, Professor of Civil Engineering at TCD, was a key figure in creating the Dublin Transport Initiative (DTI). Its central proposal was the revival of the Harcourt Street line as one of three light railway lines. Unlike previous transport plans, the DTI explicitly saw transport as part of urban revival, and what was to be revived was Dublin as – in DTI's terms – a European city. The DTI was also novel because it linked preservationists, city centre business interests and engineering academics. The focus on the new light railway gave the grouping an iconic aim. For the first time an urban initiative was not just *against* official plans, it was proposing a realistic and achievable alternative.

Significantly absent from the coalition were the established political parties, while the political left and organised labour remained completely disinterested in the broader aspects of transport questions. Paradoxically, however, the very absence of the left may have been necessary to ensure the easy involvement of business. In a way this was DTI's crucial contribution, since for the first time Dublin business interests were now positively involved in planning the regeneration of the city.

The immediate origin of the DTI was in fact a government request for advice on transport from Dublin City and County engineers. Here a key role was played by one of the engineers involved, John Henry. Only too well aware that previous plans had been drawn up by consultants who then disappeared, Henry ensured that the capacity for transport planning in the city was increased. Central to the DTI was therefore a small technical team who developed the skills of transport 'modelling' (the statistical techniques that generate traffic predictions).

In 1995 the government absorbed the DTI into a new 'Dublin Transportation Office' (DTO) with funding for permanent staff and the brief to develop transport planning for Dublin. The DTO thus inherited the transport model developed by the DTI and now has one of the most sophisticated transport models in Europe. The DTO rapidly built up expertise in transport planning, utilising existing data sources (such as Dublin Bus's ticket receipts) for the first time and stimulating the collection of new data (the 2002 national census included detailed questions on travel to work). The DTO liaised with the multitude of official bodies in the city, and by continually consulting the various interest groups it also provided a meeting point for those concerned with transport in the city.

Political sociologists sometimes use the term 'policy community' to describe an informal grouping of people who focus on a particular issue. Members of such a community have different views and institutional bases, but they share an overall problem definition. The creation of the DTO provided an institutional structure for just such a new transport 'policy community'; in the first years of the new century it contributed to the wide consensus that not only did something 'have to be done' about Dublin's traffic, but that this required investment in public transport. The DTO spearheaded the emergency plan for Dublin, the use of 'Quality Bus Corridors', which, long before Luas or the heavy rail improvements came on stream, began to create a new image for public transport in the city. In 2000 the DTO published its programme for action. 'Platform for Change' proposed a fully-costed integrated transport system for the city based on the 'vision' of Dublin as a European city

Dublin's rapid population growth was already making 'Platform for Change' out of date by the time it appeared.

Yet since then the DTO has disappeared from the political landscape and has produced no subsequent overall plan of its own. Indeed, the government's 'Transport 21' plan announced in 2005 is essentially a list of items cherry-picked from 'Platform for Change', with no recognition of the expansion of the city and the extent to which the infrastructure deficit has worsened over the last five years. Meanwhile, the DTO prefers to work behind the scenes. Like so much of the 'partnership' strand of Irish politics, it has become another government-sponsored lobby group – lobbying other bits of government.

The absorption of the DTI into the DTO has on balance probably weakened environmental and especially transport pressure groups in the city. At the moment the landscape is fairly bare. A small group of rail enthusiasts created 'Platform 11' to lobby for the use of the Phoenix Park tunnel as a passenger link, for one of the astonishing features of Dublin is that there exists an unused rail link from the West of the city through to the port. Platform 11 has managed to gain some media attention and made a presentation to the Oireachtas Joint Committee on Transport in April 2003. They are an increasingly ambitious group with an effective website[5]. Paradoxically they themselves have now become convinced that re-opening the Phoenix Park line is less important since this would merely dump traffic into the already overcrowded Connolly Station approaches. Instead they now support Irish Rail's proposed 'interconnector' underground line linking Heuston via Pearse Street and the Point with the Belfast line – the line is at the centre of Transport 21 and one that they themselves originally opposed as over-expensive and unnecessary. Above all they provide constructive and well-informed criticism of Irish Rail's curious combination of engineering competence and organisational sloth.

Other lobby groups are now thin on the ground. There is a 'Dublin Cycling Campaign' and it is represented on bodies such as the Dublin Transport Passenger Forum. Although cycling facilities are now better than a few years ago, cycling remains marginal in the city. There are no lobby groups campaigning for the welfare of pedestrians, and no organisations of parents concerned with children's safety.

The contribution of the universities is also remarkably limited. In fact, university management's obsession with 'international research' and peer-refereed publications probably ensures that staff are decreasingly able or willing to play the sort of committed social role so ably taken by Simon Perry before his death. Government research funding enabled the creation of the 'Urban Studies Institute' in UCD and the 'National Institute for Regional and Spatial Analysis' at NUI Maynooth; TCD has a 'Centre for Transport Research and Innovation for People' in its Engineering School, focussed on transport modelling and based around some EU contracts gained by Professor Margaret O'Mahony before her appointment as head of the new Dublin Transport Authority. Such centres certainly do ensure some expertise is available which did not exist in the country ten years ago, but unfortunately none has made any noticeable contribution to public debate.

Much more important are business groups. While it is an article of faith amongst business representatives that low taxes are crucial for economic growth, the employers' federation IBEC has continually called for action on public transport, pointing out the infrastructural deficit while blithely ignoring that that is in part the result of those same low tax policies. The Dublin City Centre Business Association represents property owners and retail tenants in the city centre. Interviewed for the SceneSusTech project in 1999, its chief executive Tom Coffey remarked, 'We are the old family merchant traders of Dublin.' As he explained then, the DCCBA was very much involved in the DTI given its overall orientation towards the city:

'We also have a policy of Dublin City Centre as a medieval city where we want to maintain the business and residential life of the city. We have a policy of conserving the city centre. So even though we are business people, we are very strong environmentalists as well. We see it as part of the same package.'

He said that the DCCBA was firmly behind the Luas project:

'We want an overground rail because it is safer, it is more people friendly, it is better for children, it is better for women, it is better for mobility impaired and it is better for shoppers and it is better for tourists... I have no doubt in my mind that an underground is a better technical solution but we are not building this for the technocrats. We are building it for ordinary people who will use it. You can't build an underground in a city of less than five million people and make it pay. In 2050 maybe... We needed light rail last year.'

Yet since those days the DCCBA has become less involved in transport issues, not least because its members now are also operating in the expanding suburban shopping malls. Keeping the city centre alive is no longer a life and death issue for the DCCBA.

The Dublin Chamber of Commerce also signed up to the original DTI 1994 report. However, as the on-street Luas solution became more controversial the DCC began to vacillate. For business interests a key problem with the overground solution was the level of disruption that construction would cause, yet they hardly complained that during this period the streets were continually being ripped up by the new private telecom companies. In fact, the success of the first two Luas lines has already created a situation in which private developers are prepared to support extending the lines. Being near to the Luas is already a selling point for new apartments and estate agents are noticing a 'Luas pre-

mium' on such housing. The planned extension of the
Green Line to Cherrywood and the Red Line to CityWest
will therefore probably also involve a contribution from
developers who will benefit from the lines. In this sense,
Luas shows how the public and private sectors can work
together for a planned city – and in a manner perhaps more
reminiscent of the Wide Streets Commission of 18th
Century Dublin than the developer-led development which
has characterised so much of late 20th century Dublin.

Public transport would appear to be an obvious campaigning issue for left wing parties and trade unions. Dublin's
transport crisis, so one might think, highlights the ineffectiveness of clientelist government and the consequences of
putting narrow private interests before any public good. In
fact, the left has never put public transport onto its political
agenda. Public transport in Dublin has never been an issue
that identified the political left and has never even been the
focus of any distinctive party policy. Equally, the trade union
movement totally failed to raise anything more than transport workers' wages until the issue of privatisation emerged.
Here the story is ambiguous. On the one hand government
has now slowed down its drive to privatise Dublin Bus and
open its routes to competition, but on the other hand the
unions have hardly campaigned seriously in public on the
issue, and this despite what appears to be a growing public
scepticism over the alleged benefits of privatisation.

Conversely, there is no clear public 'car lobby', even
though one is sometimes claimed to exist. Thus the
Automobile Association also signed up to the DTI and has
argued for better public transport in the city in order to give
motorists a choice. The Society of the Irish Motor Industry
(SIMI) – which is in fact the car importers' lobby – does not
seem to need to do anything to further stoke the public's
desire to purchase cars. Toll roads – and above all the notorious traffic jams on the M50 at the Westlink toll bridge –
are becoming an issue, but restrictions on cars in the city

have not produced any serious political backlash. The fact that Ireland does not have a 'car party', as briefly emerged in Switzerland (Betz, 1994), may show that Irish car owners – the vast majority of the population – recognise that most people would benefit if there were some restrictions on car usage. Alternatively, it could simply indicate that to date the supremacy of the car has not been effectively challenged!

Public visibility is not the same as political influence, particularly when, as in Dublin, so many decisions are made in ways that are unaccountable or simply untraceable. The weakness of Dublin's local authorities and the continued intervention of national government in local affairs contribute to making political decision-making in the city peculiarly murky. Sometimes public controversies occur in one area, while more important changes just happen in another area. Thus, whether or not the Luas would be built and the why and wherefore of its cost overrun were discussed continually in the media, yet the decision to franchise the operation of the line attracted very little discussion. At the same time the national motorway building programme went ahead at breakneck speed but with hardly any public discussion, despite the enormous increases in the National Roads Authority budget. Equally, the decisions of individual developers shape the city far more than all the strategic plans, but their role only attracts occasional attention, as when one of their number appears at a tribunal. Finally, the role of the construction industry itself is unclear, even though it is an obvious major beneficiary of major public infrastructure projects.

The very emptiness of this political landscape highlights the role of a few individuals such as Deirdre Kelly and Simon Perry, both now dead, and above all the campaigning journalism of Frank McDonald. Thanks to them, and not to the established political parties, there is a transport policy community, however weak. And largely thanks to them, Dublin's public transport is on the political agenda.

DUBLIN: 'EUROPEAN CITY'?

From sometime in the mid-1980s, the notion of Dublin as a 'European city' began to serve as a kind of shorthand for a new vision of the city. This meant that for the first time since the 18th century a positive image of Dublin was articulated *within Ireland*.

By the 1980s the 'malling of America' (Kowinski, 1985) had ensured that American cities were becoming 'edge cities'. Housing, employment and leisure facilities were dispersed over a wide metropolitan region (Garreau, 1991), while the city centre became abandoned and even dangerous. In the USA suburbanisation had been based on the private motorcar from the 1920s onwards, ensuring that urban sprawl occurred away from any public transport. It appeared that if nothing was done, this was the future of Dublin.

For critics of sprawl the alternative was a 'living' city centre. Such a 'European' city meant a functioning city centre with good architecture, attractive public space and upmarket retail outlets. It meant casual sociability and pavement cafés modelled on French boulevards or Italian piazzas. And European cities did in fact offer a different model of urbanisation than that into which Dublin now seemed to be entering. In Europe mass motorisation had occurred later than the USA (and later also than in Britain); the city centres remained viable, not least because of the continued public investment in public transport.

Images of the European city tended to appeal to some essential European urban nature, ignoring the rather fragile basis for this difference in particular (and always reversible) planning laws and transport policy. They also ignored the massive destruction of the *European* urban fabric that had occurred in post World War II Europe – the new brutalism of 'social housing' (British tower blocks, French *cités*), the destruction of 19th century symbols such as London's Euston Arch or Paris's Les Halles (Judt, 2005: 386), to say nothing of the horrors of state socialist buildings all across Eastern Europe. Despite these limitations, by the time of the first DTI manifesto, it was plausible that Dublin as a 'European' city meant a city that protected its historic fabric, developed the city centre as a recreational and retail centre, and in which expansion did not mean unrestrained suburban sprawl. In this 'living city' it was clear that public transport played a key role, although what exactly this involved remained unclear.

When in 1985 the Dublin in Crisis conference appealed to Jacques Delors to save Dublin from its own councillors, they were demonstrating how 'Europe' had become a metaphor for a more enlightened Ireland. Yet while the appeal of the European centre was undoubtedly strengthened by Ireland's membership of the European Union, we shall now see that actual EU policies have had very little direct impact on Dublin.

The initial Luas proposal from the DTI was made in 1993 and this became part of the 1994-1999 National Development Plan as a three branch system (lines from Tallaght, Dundrum and Ballymun to the city centre) for which IR£200m of EU funds were allocated. However, the continued chopping and changing by Fianna Fáil governments meant that it was only in 1998 that a final decision to proceed was made, ensuring that by this time some EU funds were simply lost and others had been re-allocated – to roads. Indeed, during the 1990s roads were by the far the largest beneficiaries of EU funds on physical infrastructure. Certainly, the current National Development Plan has shifted both national and EU funds towards public transport. Looking back, however, what is remarkable is the extent to which, even when 'free' money was available from outside the country to fund public transport improvements, this was one of the few areas where not all the money available was even used. Furthermore, although the extra money undoubtedly made it easier to fund public transport improvements, there is no evidence that the greater expenditure on public transport was promoted from Brussels. Here at least, 'Europe' turns out to have little to do with turning Dublin into a more European city!

Membership of the EU could have been expected to strengthen city-level political power. Many academic commentators claim that today the nation state is 'hollowed out' as power moves up to supranational organisations (like the EU) and down to sub-national entities (such as regions or cities). There is even talk of the EU as involving a 'Europe of cities'. In Ireland, however, the reality is very different: the EU has hardly enabled Dublin or the Dublin region to become more powerful. In fact central government has continually ensured that Ireland has pulled down EU 'regional' funds – without any serious shift to local or regional accountability.

Certainly the EU does include an advisory Council of the Regions, now renamed the Council of the Regions and Cities, and this does potentially provide a channel of communication between cities and regions that does not depend on 'their' governments. Some EU initiatives have been directed specifically at cities, such as the 'Sustainable Cities' programme and the environmental programme 'Agenda 21'. Yet these formal political structures and programmes are probably less important as a channel for mutual learning than the professional associations of planners and even architects.

EU AND PRIVATISATION

In a rather vague way, Ireland's EU membership has over the years promoted ideas of sustainability within the city. If only very indirectly, 'Europe' has created a climate of ideas which has favoured public transport. However, the effect of the EU on the organisation of Dublin's public transport is now much more direct, and much less straightforwardly beneficial.

Historically public transport in Europe, unlike in much of the USA, has been provided by various forms of public enterprises, owned either by the state or by the local authority, subsidised directly from national or local funds, and protected by various restrictions on competitors entering their market. Each element – public ownership, subsidy and regulation – is anathema to those who believe in the virtues of the market.

The European 'common market' is defined as the free movement of goods, capital, labour and services within Europe. In the case of goods, equal competition meant of course not just the abolition of tariffs, but also of subsidies. Accordingly, state enterprises were always suspect in the eyes of the Commission. As the economy has shifted away from manufacturing to services, so state-owned service enterprises such as public transport undertakings have become more of an issue. Today the opening of service markets such as transport has become a self-reinforcing process: as private companies have been allowed to enter these markets, companies such as Connex and Stagecoach have developed. But their expansion depends on absorbing other new entrants and above all on other markets becoming open to them.

While a 'common market' was in principle always potentially going to threaten state enterprises, they were protected by a contradictory principle, the recognition that they provided so-called 'Services of General Interest'. For a long time this was taken as justifying not only state subsidy but outright state ownership. Since the late 1980s, however, both Commission policy and, even more importantly, decisions by the European Court of Justice (ECJ), have increasingly attempted to open these services to competition. For example, in every European country the post office not only delivered and collected the mail, but also usually in every locality provided government services such as paying out welfare benefits and pensions. The state had an effective monopoly on the delivery of mail and postal workers were government employees. The post office might or might not make a notional profit, but its role was to ensure a national service, so that everyone, no matter where they lived, had essentially the same service. Getting the post – and later getting a telephone – was as much a right of citizens as a service bought by consumers. In some countries the post office was the friendly face of the state; in others, such as Italy, it was a by-word for bureaucratic incompetence. However, the post office was unquestionably a key part of the state administration everywhere, a key link between the state and the citizens. Now a series of ECJ judgements have forced states to abandon their monopoly and to make their post offices behave like any other commercial enterprise, with the obvious consequence that mail services are being privatised all over Europe.

Compared with areas such as electricity and even the post, it has been rather difficult to introduce 'competition' into many areas of transport. Even when privately owned, railways were with very few exceptions unitary enterprises that owned both the track and the trains that ran on it. European railways were state owned partly because of their military or economic importance, but also because competition between lines was seen to be wasteful without usually providing any better service to the customer. Indeed, one argument for state ownership had been the way in which competition between companies prevented any integration of their services.

Contemporary attempts to privatise state owned railways have involved treating the railway infrastructure (above all the track) and the operations (i.e. the trains) as separate accounting units. It thus becomes possible to treat the railway track as a 'network' to which any company should be allowed access on which to run its own trains.

Thus a 1991 European directive insisted on the separation of infrastructure and operations in accounting terms. In principle such a measure enables 'transparent' accounting, identifying exactly what is being subsidised and enabling one or both enterprises to be privatised. Nonetheless, this has been very slow to be enforced, so that for example the French SNCF was not even divided into two separate accounting units until 2004. As chapter 7 has already shown, once these accounting units become separate companies this creates rather obvious problems of safety, as well as enormous accounting and legal costs.

Arguably the Commission's obsession with privatisation has actually detracted from any attempt to create a genuinely integrated European railway system. There has been some progress towards common safety standards, but inter-operability remains difficult (e.g. the French TGV and German high speed trains use different traction systems) and unusual outside the Thalys/Eurostar network of London-Paris-Brussels-Amsterdam-Köln. Despite the fact that its dense network of cities makes much of Western Europe an ideal terrain for high speed train services, the major change in travel over the last decade has been the explosion of budget airlines who, just like car owners, manage to avoid paying for the environmental damage they cause.

Against this background it is perhaps not surprising that EU policy for urban public transport has been more concerned with creating markets for private companies than with creating sustainable cities for European citizens. The policy objective is clear: to ensure that municipally or state owned transport undertakings are treated like private enterprises. If they receive subsidies then these must be for designated services for which in principle other 'providers' could compete. At the moment this has not been enforced across Europe, so that Dublin Bus remains both part of a state owned company and the recipient of a generalised subsidy. Indeed, in 2005 the European Parliament voted that state enterprises with regional monopolies could continue to exist, but would be barred from competing for other business outside of their area.

These legal changes ensure that public transport across Europe is increasingly provided by private companies. Here companies such as Connex or Stagecoach can develop economies of scope and scale, which often ensures that they are far more cost-effective than a small locally owned company could ever be, quite apart from the fact that they will usually have much easier access to capital than even the largest state enterprise. Indeed, the importance of the market for public transport within Europe is providing Connex with a secure basis for its global expansion. However, the worry is that these gains could be short-term, and that the end of state ownership of public transport means that public transport could disappear much more easily if the political climate changed. Private companies have little long-term interest in an integrated network and private ownership was one reason for the collapse of public transport systems in the USA.

Notes:

1   At the time of the study London's success was largely the historical legacy of an extensive suburban underground and overground railway network consolidated in the 1930s.

2   As Bob Kiley remarked in 1999 in a speech to a UK government seminar on devolution before he became London's Commissioner for Transport: 'What on earth made you think devolution could work unless the regional government is given the ability to raise taxes? In the US, 65 per cent of taxes are raised at local level' (Wolmar, 2001: 163).

3   This weakness was explored in detail in the research project 'UNIREG – Universities in Regional Development' funded by the European Commission. Detailed reports are available at

www.tcd.ie/erc/pastprojectunireg.php; see also Boucher et al (2003) for a comparative discussion of the Dublin situation.

4   British recognition of the UCD degree was crucial since most students at the time expected to emigrate to work in Britain. Speech by Ruari Quinn at opening of UCD Urban Institute, 23 June 2004.

5   http://www.platform11.org

Chapter 9

Dublin: looking over the edge of the precipice?

In European terms Dublin is a relatively extreme version of a car city. Car usage is high and car dependency is increasing. The private car has been built into the fabric of the city, while public transport has become more and more inadequate. High levels of car usage ensure Ireland makes its own national contribution to global environmental disaster. Since more cars simply generate more gridlock, Dubliners' reliance on the private car is destroying their ability to move around their city. Much less discussed but arguably even more fundamental: car dependency produces social exclusion and car usage undermines social cohesion. While governments obsess about privatisation, they have not addressed the institutional deficits, which in fact block any solution to the problem.

This characterisation may seem overly pessimistic. Not only has spending on public transport infrastructure increased in the last few years, but with the new Dublin Transport Authority there is surely at last one organisation in charge of the capital's transport. In fact Dublin is now on a knife edge: the city's mobility could go either way. This chapter begins by exploring the different possibilities, using some scenarios developed during the SceneSusTech project.

As the second part of the chapter argues, while Dublin's rush to ever increasing car dependency may have been slowed, much more active policy will be needed to reverse the trend. The chapter ends with three sections of 'bullet points' that could form the basis for real change in Dublin. They involve urban transport policy in its broadest sense, the governance of the city, and above all, the linkage between urban transport and urban citizenship.

DUBLIN ON THE KNIFE EDGE: POSSIBLE SCENARIOS

One vision of Dublin's future – probably the most likely one – is that many things will get worse because the direction of change will remain the same. This 'business as usual' scenario means that Dublin continues on its present path towards ever-greater car dependency. There is only one mode of mobility – the car.

In this first vision the suburbs expand out of reach of public transport; more and more retail centres and office parks can only be reached by private car; as the city disperses car ownership becomes essential even for those living in the city centre. Not only does Dublin become a metropolitan region spreading over most of the old Pale but this sprawl lacks any coherence. It is 'edge city' – a nowhere place. Such a dispersed city region is environmentally unsustainable because it is a resource-intensive system and may turn out to be a dinosaur, unable to adapt to a new global environment of energy shortages.

In this scenario the Luas is certainly there and the two lines have probably been connected. The port tunnel is working and there may be fewer heavy lorries in the city centre. Indeed, there may even be a metro line linking the city centre to the airport. These prestige projects ensure that the city centre remains attractive enough and accessible enough to serve as a recreational centre and tourist destination. However, the city centre is an island in a vast suburban sprawl, for expanding the rail network for inhabitants has been defined as too expensive compared with a single line to the airport for visitors.

In this scenario the Interconnector – the tunnel proposed in *Transport 21* to enable trains to travel from Heuston Station via St. Stephen's Green to a new Docklands station – remains just another fading line on a map. Officially the reason is that the Department of Finance has discovered that it was not cost effective, although there are rumours that government was determined to prevent the construction of any new lines that could not be easily operated by private sector franchises. In this scenario public transport is increasingly marginal, even for the journey to work. While more and more people work in the suburbs, public transport only serves those who live near a transport corridor in the suburbs and work in the city centre. Public transport resources are also used inefficiently, since journeys are mostly in one direction at the start of the day and in the other direction at the end of the day.

In this world a few new state bodies have been created to tackle the transport problem, but the growing number of institutions simply mirrors the growing number of cars – and like the cars they increasingly only get in each others' way. There continues to be no political will to devolve power to the city; local politics remain mired in clientelist trivia; regional politics simply do not exist; no elected politician has a vision of the city. Appeals to privatisation, competition and the market take the place of any attempt to maintain, integrate and develop a transport network for the whole city. Certainly, the latest public infrastructure projects have been rather better implemented than the initial Luas or M50, since at last more risks have been transferred to the contractors. However, no real expertise has been built up within either the engineering community or in central government, so Dublin remains an easy target for private construction companies and transport 'providers'.

In the first vision car dependency has become a fact of life for nearly all of the metropolitan region's citizens. An alternative vision reverses this trend. Car usage is restrained, both because of reduced demand for car-type journeys (more needs are met locally) and there are more alternatives to the car. The city is a *multi-modal* city.

Public transport in this vision is not just about the point-to-point 'transit' from the suburb or airport to the city centre; it is both multi-modal and multi-functional. In the urban core a dense grid of transport (bus, tram, and metro, supplemented by widely available private taxis) expands the pavement city described in Chapter 2. The city centre itself has new world-class public spaces linking its major cultural attractions. In this part of the city more and more needs can be met without using a car, and interestingly, new needs develop which are not based on the car. In this vision multi-modal and multi-functional public transport makes mobility without a car the rational choice within the city core, and perfectly possible within an area roughly contained by the current boundaries of Dublin City Council.

In this second vision public transport resources are used more efficiently, since the city centre is only the largest of a series of urban cores in what has now become a polycentric city. Such cores are not only interlinked public transport nodes but themselves urban centres in which short trips without a car have again become feasible. Suburban centres are town centres, not just shopping malls. Even in the suburbs housing is no longer only the standard suburban house and garden, but includes (as can in fact already be seen in Dublin today) higher density forms such as high quality apartments. Everywhere increased provision of local facilities reduces the necessity of car journeys and increases the number of walking journeys.

In this second vision suburbs have been 'retro-fitted'

and hence begin to have high population densities ('densification'). Nonetheless, in the outer suburbs car usage remains far higher than in the (expanded) city core. Indeed, the gap between city centre and suburbs has actually increased, since transport change has been more dramatic in the (expanded) city centre. Yet this gap itself simply indicates that choice has become possible. Firstly, there are now more areas in which using a car is a genuine choice, since here using a car is no longer essential for normal social interaction. Secondly, the extension of such areas means that more people can now genuinely choose whether to live a car-dependent lifestyle or not, rather than being compelled to live in an area in which using a car is a precondition for a normal existence.

Such a transformed city depends not just on transport innovation: it is impossible to imagine without *institutional innovation*. In this vision therefore the DTA has become a real authority with power over transport; it plans and co-ordinates an integrated network and enforces continual improvements in the services which it funds. Crucially, it also has power over land use planning and so increasingly ensures that development is linked to transport facilities. It can exercise power because it has democratic legitimation derived from its accountability to an elected metropolitan government. Since such a metropolitan government has real power, it in turn attracts politicians with vision and verve who have built their political career by transforming Dublin and who are now identified with the city's success. The city's dynamism and the city government's legitimacy enable the city government, largely through the DTA, to cajole and if necessary threaten private developers into a strategy which is compatible with the new vision of the city, concentrating large developments at transport nodes. Indeed, as these new forms of building become successful, private enterprise begins to work with the city rather than against it.

How feasible are such alternatives? In order to explore the possible developments in transport policy, in the final stage of the SceneSusTech project we held meetings with a group of transport experts (planners, academics and journalists) in each case study city. We asked the experts in each case study city to visualise their city in twenty-five years time. In order to capture the different aspects of policy involved, and also in order to make systematic comparisons between the cities, we used a modified version of a transport policy scenario model developed by Nijkamp and his colleagues (Nijkamp et al, 1998).

This so-called spider model is based on the assumption that transport systems involve a number of *inter-related* policy aspects. We asked the experts how they saw the future of their city on eight different policy dimensions, grouped into four different aspects: spatial, economic, institutional and social. Each dimension involves a continuum between two extreme positions. For example, the spatial aspect of the transport scenario includes the dimension of *urban form*. Here one extreme would be the highly concentrated and high-density *compact city*, at the other extreme would be the more dispersed, suburbanized and *diffuse city*. Experts were asked to indicate their views with a numerical score on each dimension, so that for example a score of '1' on the urban form dimension meant a completely compact city, a score of '5' an entirely suburbanized city. Each group of experts was asked to score their cities twice, firstly in terms of what they themselves *wanted* to happen, and then in terms of what they realistically *expected* to happen (Figure 9.1).

In terms of the role of the city within each country, the experts expected to see urban development concentrated in the major conurbations, rather than in 'chains and zones' as they would have preferred. Taken overall, their hopes and expectations broadly coincided on the dimension of 'urban form', although the chart masks the fact that the Dublin group expected their city to become much more diffuse than they wished. On the other dimensions the experts tended to expect a move towards market regulation, private provision, profit orientation and market principles in public transport, even though in general they were not convinced that this was actually desirable. Equally they anticipated that their cities would generate more social exclusion and more individualism than they would have preferred.

Figure 9.1 Experts in four cities: expected and desired scenarios

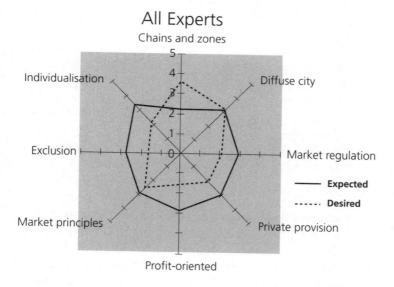

All Experts

Source: *SceneSusTech, Expert focus groups*

In a second part of this stage of the research, we then asked the experts to evaluate specific transport policies and technologies in the same manner. Here the experts were particularly supportive of rail-based technologies (tram, metro and heavy rail) and of new environmentally friendly cars (Figure 9.2). Conversely, they were less supportive of ring roads and road widening, although they expected that these were very likely to actually happen.

Figure 9.2 Experts in four cities: expected and desired technologies

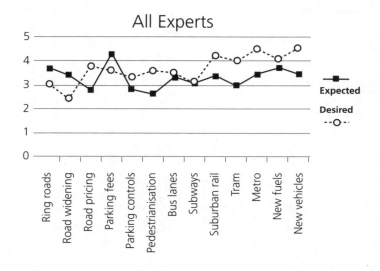

Source: *SceneSusTech, Expert focus groups*

All in all, the findings are pessimistic. The experts are all fairly clear what measures are needed to reduce car usage and improve mobility. They stress an overall institutional framework that focuses on public provision and gives *relatively* little weight to market principles; they favour rail-based solutions rather than new roads or even mechanisms to regulate car usage such as road pricing or parking fees. Overall their desired city appears to be a compact 'European' city. Yet what they expect will happen is almost the mirror image of this: institutional frameworks that opt for private provision and that attempt to achieve policy objectives through market mechanisms, road widening and even road building rather than rail-based mass transit, and, although the evidence is perhaps less clear on this, continued suburbanisation.

Another striking point of agreement between the experts is what they did *not* discuss. Although the dimensions of the scenario building exercise focused strongly on issues of market versus state regulation and provision, such questions did not particularly concern the experts. Privatisation, deregulation, competitive tendering for public service contracts – all the institutional innovations that attract so much attention at national and EU level – all played relatively little role in the open-ended discussions. In other words, such 'solutions' appear to these experts to be at best marginal and at worst irrelevant to actually tackling the transport issue in their cities.

POLICY PERSPECTIVES

The scenario building exercise suggested that the most realistic prognosis for Dublin's future is 'business as normal'. Unlike ten years ago, however, 'business as normal' does now include some new public transport projects. Change it seems is possible and actual policy has moved closer to the views of our experts than they themselves anticipated. However, the contrast between the two visions shows that merely decorating the city centre with a few trams is not enough to change the quality of life for the citizens as a whole; it certainly is not enough to push the city region onto a more sustainable transport path. This section now outlines what that would involve.

First, two disclaimers are needed. The aim of this section – let alone of this book – is *not* to plead for particular infrastructure projects. It does not pretend to adjudicate between, for example, different proposed Luas lines. The growing awareness of the transport problem over the last decade has meant that almost all Dubliners – and many people outside of Dublin – have their own pet solution to the transport problem. There is nothing wrong with such popular involvement, not least because it shows that Dubliners now care about the possible forms of mobility in their city. However, the purpose of the book is rather different. It is to argue the importance of public transport and indeed of a public transport *system* in general, rather than to plead for particular transport measures.

For rather similar reasons, the reader will look in vain for costings of transport proposals, let alone for cost benefit analyses of particular transport options. Costs and benefits are crucial in particular policy decisions, but the unrelenting focus on economic costs in transport discussion in Dublin is in fact part of the problem rather than the solution. One reason why we have ended up with such a transport disaster in Dublin has been because transport decisions have been discussed in narrow economic terms. Ultimately the decision for or against public transport does not depend on the particular outcomes of cost benefit analysis, for it is a question of the form of life we want to lead and the sort of city in which we want to live. To claim that transport issues can be resolved by technical discussions comprehensible only to economic experts is absurd – as absurd as claiming that economic equations can enable us to decide between adherence to the Catholic or Protestant religions, or between democratic or dictatorial forms of government. Certainly such questions have economic dimensions, but they ultimately involve choices between values. They are decisions we all have to make, and in which we are all expert. To make such decisions dependent on the outcome of technical calculations is ultimately to abdicate individual political responsibility.

Whether or not people buy cars, whether or not people

use cars, how people use cars – all of these issues depend in part upon their immediate social and geographical context. At its simplest, individual car ownership is essential in a car dependent suburb; it is an option where there is good public transport and plentiful local facilities. This suggests that as a general principle, contextual measures (specific traffic restrictions transport, specific transport alternatives) are more effective than general measures (increasing fuel taxes, even road pricing).

Today transport politics involve a paradox. On the one hand there is now in European cities a widespread acceptance that mobility based on the private car is unsustainable (and indeed unpleasant for the user as well as the environment). Consequently most European citizens accept that they cannot always be allowed to use their cars in the way they might like, and that alternatives (from walking to public transport) should be encouraged. On the other hand there is also the pervasive belief that people will not accept restrictions on car usage, and most people believe that their cars are absolutely essential to their ordinary lives. In this situation traffic control measures may call on a vague fund of goodwill when they are proposed in the abstract, but may also be passionately resented when they are actually applied.

Effective policy therefore needs to deliver clear benefits to at least some of those whose freedom it restrains. At its simplest this means that there is no point in restraining car access to city centres ('sticks') unless people can see benefits ('carrots'). Such benefits can range from pleasant pedestrian piazzas to clean and reliable public transport. Without such benefits transport politics become *all sticks but no carrots*. For example, it would be technically feasible to introduce some form of congestion charging for the area between the canals in Dublin, but this would be a political disaster unless there had been a prior improvement in public transport. Car users would be punished for using their cars, but not offered any plausible alternative.

Without such alternatives, sustainable transport policy simply becomes a dead-end, stimulating demands for motorists' 'rights' for greater use of their cars, and possibly even producing political parties committed to 'cars' rights' (as has happened, for example, in Holland and Switzerland). Yet such rights can hardly be unlimited. Nobody for example suggests that car owners should have the right to drive on whichever side of the road they please, since the benefits of *enforced* adherence to the rules of the road are fairly clear. Effective transport policy has to make the benefits of other constraints equally clear[1].

KEY ELEMENTS OF URBAN TRANSPORT POLICY

Against this background, it is now possible to indicate what needs to be done – or at the least the basic objectives of policy. As we shall see, merely building metros or whatever is only part of what is needed. Beyond such basic 'hard' principles of transport engineering and urban planning, there exists what could be called a set of 'soft' principles in which transport and planning become almost aspects of social policy. Developing good urban transport has to be linked to issues of public safety, to increasing local rather than city-level mobility, to developing a culture of public transport use and to improving urban design.

Transport Engineering and urban planning

Taken as a whole, there is no longer any mystery as to the measures required to reduce car usage and car dependency within European cities (e.g. Pucher, 1998; for more qualified statement, Stokes, 1996). In a car dependent city there is only one way to move around – by car. Ensuring that it is possible for people to choose to live without a car means that people have genuine choice over where to go and how to get there. The move towards the *multi-modal city* requires:

High quality public transport, including innovative low cost solutions and an extensive and safe taxi service. To reduce overall car dependency, as opposed to merely altering the 'modal split' on specific point-to-point routes, such transport has to form an integrated transport grid combining different transport modes (bus, tram, metro, surface rail). In general public transport should be prioritised over road construction, which tends to simply generate more car traffic.

A priority for all of Greater Dublin: build the Interconnector first

The Interconnector is the proposed underground link from the south-western suburban railway line at Heuston Station to the northern suburban railway line via St. Stephen's Green, Pearse Station and the Docklands. The Interconnector would for the first time integrate all Dublin suburban rail services. It would enable fast DART type services across much of the Greater Dublin Area and thus benefit the whole city. It would turn Dublin's rail system into an equivalent of the fast suburban rail systems of Paris or Madrid. It is included in 'Transport 21' but only scheduled for completion at the end of the programme in 2015.

Effective land use planning, ensuring that main traffic generators (employment, hospitals, shopping areas, airports, etc.) are located on public transport nodes. Particularly important, and particularly difficult to ensure, is the regulation of large-scale retail outlets, since their continued growth is usually at the cost of local shops, which can be reached on foot, and of existing urban centres, which are usually well served by public transport.

Physical restrictions on cars in city centre areas, including the reduction of off street parking and above all, the banning of private cars from large areas of the urban core. Multi-storey car parks in the city centre only generate more traffic and should be phased out as public transport access improves.

Prioritise pedestrians over cars and create attractive new urban spaces. Improve pavements and street furniture; lengthen pedestrian crossing times at stop lights. Improve facilities for cyclists.

Create a Dublin city centre showpiece

Trinity College Dublin and the old Houses of Parliament (now the Bank of Ireland) at College Green are two of Dublin's most beautiful 18th century buildings; round the corner in Nassau Street is the new entrance to the National Gallery. All are major tourist destinations – currently linked by a busy traffic-filled road. Why not pedestrianise the whole area? This would create a world-class urban space in the middle of Dublin as good as the famous Campo in Sienna, which forty years ago was also a traffic round-about. Meet you for coffee on College Green?

Public transport and public safety

Public transport, so Chapter 7 argued, is both a form of public space (when we use a bus or a train we are in a public place) and contributes to the creation of public spaces (the pavements as spaces which we all can use). This can only happen if such spaces are *safe*. This has three aspects:

Make pedestrian spaces safe. Re-urbanisation assumes that inner city areas can be made attractive residential areas, in particular for relatively affluent professional groups who value cultural facilities and even social diversity. In Dublin and elsewhere, pedestrianisation has been used to regain some areas of the city from the private car. However, this can often ignore that the attractiveness of such areas is undermined by the extent to which they are often seen as particularly unsafe. Thus the SceneSusTech results showed that the Centro Storico of Bologna – the showpiece city centre of the study – had the *lowest* score of all our 12 localities for perceived personal safety. In cities of controlled car dependency, the city centre has a particularly emblematic role. It is therefore imperative that it is not allowed to degenerate into a 'dangerous zone' which people avoid.

Make the streets safe. More generally our results suggest that one reason people use cars is because they feel physically protected by the car from random violence outside. Making streets safe – and perceived to be safe – therefore reduces one basis for car dependency. To get citizens out of their cars, it is probably necessary that the police get out of theirs!

Make public transport safe. Similar arguments apply to public transport. Here too there is a risk of a vicious circle: public transport is seen as unsafe, so those who can use the private car abandon it, thus giving more scope to hooligans and removing more public spaces from the public as notoriously has happened in the past on some Dublin bus routes.

Developing local mobility
Much discussion of public transport is stuck in the transit

city epoch, assuming the key role of public transport is to move large numbers of people from their homes in the suburbs to their workplaces in the city centre, and usually all at about the same time. This is public transport as the rush-hour commute. Yet such journeys are a decreasing proportion of all journeys that people make, and even a declining proportion of all journeys to work. One consequence is that transport policy needs to focus on more localised forms of mobility. In particular it needs to:

Facilitate walking and cycling in low-density areas. One credo of the new urbanism is the importance of high-density housing. However, the expanding number of apartments within Dublin has not by itself had much impact on levels of car use. Conversely, relatively low-density housing areas are not necessarily extreme cases of car dependency. In these areas car dependency can be reduced by policies such as effective land and transport planning (clustering housing around transport nodes), provision of effective local transport, facilitating walking and cycling, and ensuring the maintenance of local facilities (shops, schools, health centres etc.). Even without major investments, some research shows that public health campaigns to reduce car usage in low-density areas can persuade people to walk rather than use the car.

Use public transport to enhance local mobility. Especially in inner city areas, car dependency can be best reduced by public transport that extends citizens' *local* mobility and enhances *diffuse* (not 'point to point') mobility. In this context public transport extends the physical area that people can consider within walking distance. High quality, frequent and predictable local bus services are absolutely crucial here. However, it is worth remembering that on-street light rail systems ('trams') have some specific characteristics (on-street visibility and accessibility, physically demarcated routes specified by the tracks, comfort) which help them to facilitate citizens' use of local space: the highly visible rails of the tram are the best way to bind together an area. At the moment the fact that trams are so much more expensive than buses tends to make them impractical for this role apart from in the city centre itself. However, it is worth exploring ways that light rail could once again be as 'light' as were traditional trams, rather than necessarily always being the gold-plated version we have today.

A culture of public transport use

By now it is obvious that transport policy is not just about building metros or even painting lines on roads to designate bus lanes. An effective public transport policy involves a specific way of living in the city. It has four objectives that could be called 'cultural':

Maintain and develop trust in public transport. If people are to use their cars less, they have to develop *trust* in the alternatives. Equally, public transport users are more likely to switch to cars if they lose trust in the service. The obvious implication is that industrial relations disputes in the public transport sector have a considerable knock-on effect. This should be borne in mind by public sector trade unions that wish to safeguard the employment of their members. Equally, ensuring the day-to-day reliability of the service has to be a high priority.

Maintain and develop non-car competences. Walking and cycling are also alternatives that require relatively small infrastructure investments. It is, however, important to recognise that they require not just physical facilities, but the development of 'mobility skills' and of a walking and cycling culture. Again, the safety of public spaces is both cause and effect of such skills and of such a culture.

Equally, using public transport is a skill that needs to be learnt. It can be helped by ensuring that good quality reliable information is available to all transport users.

Making car ownership a choice and not a necessity. Once people own a car, they will use it and probably develop lifestyles for which it becomes essential. However, this development is not inevitable. Studies such as SceneSusTech show how there is a wide variety of car ownership between cities and between different areas of cities. Even in some apparently car dependent areas, it is possible to find non-car owners. While politicians are unlikely to find the courage to make *reducing car ownership levels* an explicit objective, it is possible to make it an explicit objective that the car should not be essential if one is to live in a city.

Ensure that young people do not have to use a car. Given that car ownership generates car dependent activities, a policy objective should be to ensure that young adults feel able to choose *not* to have a car for as long as possible. Public transport services (routes and timetables) need to adjust to the need for other journeys apart from the traditional suburb to city centre daytime services. Here Dublin's Night Link buses are obviously important, but there is also scope for more radical innovations such as Milan's pooled bus-taxi service. Given the extent to which young adults (especially young males) are disproportionately involved in car accidents (see Chapter 4), such a policy has important health policy benefits.

Public transport and urban design
When the campaign for better public transport in Dublin began in earnest in the 1980s, a central theme was that public transport was crucial to a 'living city'. The idea of Dublin as a 'European city' has a similar resonance. The

very fact that public transport is now part of public debate in ways that it was not twenty years ago means that much discussion has now become more technically sophisticated. The Central Statistics Office (CSO) now collects detailed information on travel (especially travel to work); the DTO has developed mathematical models to predict the consequences of changes in transport infrastructure; there is the beginning of a research community of engineers, planners and different forms of social scientists. Such technical sophistication will make a crucial contribution to any transformation of Dublin's transport situation. However, while such technical discussions will be an essential part of any specific transport decision, they paradoxically may obscure the original and more fundamental objective – the role of transport in re-designing the city. Accordingly, one final and fundamental policy principle has to be:

Use public transport to enhance urban design and quality of life. Within the Anglo-Saxon technical literature, public transport evaluation focuses on cost effectiveness. Curiously absent from such expert discussion is what seemed to matter for many of the people we talked to in the SceneSusTech project, namely the quality of life in the city and even the actual cityscape itself. Choosing between an urban motorway and a light rail system is not just a choice between different modes of transport; it is a choice between different designs for the city and even between different forms of life. Many of the great 19h century cityscapes were built by engineers such as Hausmann in Paris or Cerdà in Barcelona. Whether they like it or not, transport engineers today are designers of cities just as much as – or perhaps more so than – urban planners or architects. Given the role of cities in European culture, it is imperative that such aesthetic and quality of life issues are given an explicit role in policy choices, *even if they are difficult to integrate into cost-benefit analyses.*

URBAN GOVERNANCE TO REDUCE CAR DEPENDENCY

The experts in our scenario exercises were in broad agreement on what measures were needed in their cities; the Dublin experts in particular were not convinced that these would ever be implemented. What then can be learnt from those cities that have, to some extent at least, implemented such measures?

Create a unitary transport authority. Time and time again research has shown the need for a unitary transport authority responsible for overall transport planning and management. The question of the actual ownership of transport undertakings is secondary to this. If transport is provided by enterprises owned by the national or local state, then they must be accountable to this authority and co-ordinated by it. Because Dublin has not had such an authority it has had state-owned enterprises that have only minimal co-ordination between them. Conversely, if transport is provided through some form of market, then the transport authority has to either regulate the market and/or issue service contracts. Such a transport authority is no magic bullet: its existence does not guarantee that Dublin's transport problems will be solved, but it is impossible to imagine a solution without it. Ideally, such an authority also has to play a major role in overall land use planning.

Strengthen urban government. Reducing car dependency requires effective city level governments, with some independent tax base and some democratic authority and legitimacy. This is of course in accordance with the subsidiarity principle of the European Union. Some autonomy at city level allows citizens to evaluate decisions that are made in their city. If national governments wish to improve urban transport, they need to devolve power to the cities.

Embed cities in effective regional or metropolitan level government with strategic power. Cities with effective transport policies are embedded in regional or metropolitan level governments that have strategic capacity and democratic legitimacy. This is especially important if land use planning is to be integrated with transport planning. The planning of urban public transport, in particular the crucial issue of network integration, can only be carried out at regional or metropolitan level. This requires some form of regional level transport authority responsible to a regional government with democratic legitimacy. Once again, such institutions can be developed through greater development of European Union sub-national institutions, such as in particular the Committee of the Regions as potentially strengthened by the Nice Treaty (Article 263).

European institutions should enhance the move towards subsidiarity in urban policy. A relatively autonomous city government can learn from initiatives in other European cities, not least through EU initiatives such as the sustainable cities programme. Without effective city government, such exchanges can degenerate into 'junkets' for powerless politicians, undermining the legitimacy of democratic institutions. Politicians who participate in such exchanges should be compelled to formally report to their electorates on what lessons they have learnt from such exchanges and how policy in the city will be changed as a result! In fact, there is now anecdotal evidence that European citizens themselves are informally 'benchmarking' their city governments: there is growing awareness, not least through travel and tourism, of how other cities tackle transportation issues. City governments are going to have to develop the capacity to respond to these demands, even though national politicians are usually reluctant to cede power.

Build urban coalitions. Where cities have successful transport policies these are usually constructed by policy coalitions that span major interest groups and conventional ideological divides. In Dublin the conventional parties of the left have had virtually no impact on transport policy and the role of the trade unions has been restricted to a narrow focus on the interests of their members working in CIÉ. Part of the problem has been the vicious circle of Irish local politics, where the powerlessness of local government ensures that local politics cannot attract politicians who wish to actually change their city. However, 'progressive' local politicians have not understood that transport and planning policies are successful when they create a framework within which major interests, e.g. land developers, can operate to their own advantage. It is important to be clear that this is *not* an argument for seeking to compromise with existing interests at all costs. Instead, it is about creating a new framework within which interests, *including in particular private sector interests*, can operate in a way that is compatible with the over-riding objective of sustainable development.

URBAN TRANSPORT AND URBAN CITIZENSHIP

Urban transport clearly is not just a technical issue about how people move around their city. Ultimately it involves a choice of style of life, of how one lives in a city. We should not be afraid or too cynical to acknowledge that it is also about urban citizenship – about how people live in the city, use the city and participate in the city's public life. This leads to two final principles of transport policy:

Enhance public transport as a public service. At the time of writing much transport policy discussion focuses on the issue of public versus private ownership, the possibility of using Public-Private-Partnerships (PPPs) and enhancing the role of the private sector in service delivery. In the first instance much of this debate is irrelevant. For example, at the time of the SceneSusTech research project, nearly all the public transport in the case study cities was in public ownership, yet the quality of the service ranged from the appalling (Athens, Dublin) through the competent (Bologna) to the impressive (Helsinki). More wide ranging studies have come to similar conclusions (NERA and TIS.PT, 2001). The most that could be argued is that, compared with private sector provision, publicly owned transport authorities *tend* to have better integration between transport modes, but worse industrial relations[2].

Traditionally public transport has been defined as part of the realm of 'public provision' or 'public welfare', which is excluded from EU competition law by Articles 16 and 86 of the Treaty. There is now a clear trend, partly initiated by the Commission, to reduce or even remove this protection. This is usually justified in the name of greater transparency and efficiency. Such policy ignores what is crucial, namely the coherence of the system. More fundamentally, we have seen that privatising public transport in the name of efficiency and transparency runs the risk of removing public support from public transport.

Place transport in the context of citizens' rights and obligations. Car dependency enhances social exclusion; car usage undermines social cohesion. Conversely therefore, an urban public transport system forms 'the sinews of urban citizenship' (Wickham, 2006). It is this that ultimately justifies the technical need for transport system integration. Dublin needs an integrated transport system so that its citizens can have the *right* to move around their city.

Like other forms of citizenship, 'transport citizenship' has obligations as well as rights. It imposes the obligation of 'civil' behaviour in public transport and public places; it even involves that diffused but crucial feeling that some of us have that walking, cycling or using public transport themselves involve political choices. In an epoch of environmental crisis, transport citizenship carries the key obligation of responsible mobility at the individual level. This may well mean that the privatisation of public transport undermines one ethical basis for alternatives to the private motorcar. It definitely means that transport policy is ultimately central to the way we live our lives. If Dublin is to have citizens rather than simply inhabitants, if Ireland is to have a capital city of which it can be proud, one cause and effect will be a move towards a more sustainable and more *public* form of mobility within the entire city.

Notes:

1   In the USA citizens enjoy the right to bear arms, a 'right' that most Europeans would regard as needing to be restrained in order to ensure fewer people are killed. Restraining car owners raises similar gains and losses. Such mutual acceptance of restraint is an example of the civilising process (Elias, 1995), which in these terms appears more advanced in Europe than the USA.

2   Even such generalisations are hardly cast-iron: Dublin has relatively bad industrial relations *and* poor integration.

Appendix

The SceneSusTech Project

Part of the pressure for better public transport in Dublin comes from the awareness that in some other cities things are done better. Appropriately therefore, much of the research underlying this book derived from the EU-funded research project SceneSusTech – 'Scenarios for Sustainable Technology: Car-Systems in the city and the sociology of embedded technologies'. This was a comparative study of four European cities: Athens, Bologna, Dublin and Helsinki.

Of the four cities, two – Athens and Dublin – were chosen as examples of cities apparently dominated by the private car; the two other cities – Bologna and Helsinki – were chosen as cities where public transport seemed more effective. The project began with an initial literature review, focusing in particular on the environmental implications of car usage. We then compared our four cities to other cities in the world by adding information about them to a data set compiled by an Australian research team on transport usage for 37 world cities in 1990 (Kenworthy et al, 1997).

The next stage of the research attempted to explain how Athens and Dublin have become car dependent and conversely how Bologna and Helsinki have become cities that constrain car dependency. In each city this involved a historical analysis of the 'technological trajectory' of the car system and a political sociology of contemporary transport and planning decisions.

The research not only compared the four cities, it also 'zoomed in' to compare three areas within *each* city – a standard middle class suburban area, a working class suburban area, and a 'gentrified' inner city area (Table A.1). If a city such as Dublin has bad public transport, what effect does this have on, for example, a relatively deprived working class area of Tallaght *compared with a similar area in Helsinki?* Such comparisons would show, so we hoped, the effect of city level decisions on transport on the lives of different people. Within each of these areas we carried out a questionnaire-based social survey, ethnographic observation and also held focus groups with residents.

Table A.1 Four cities, twelve areas

In italics: abbreviation used in charts

	Working class peripheral	Middle class peripheral	Inner city professional
Athens	Agioi Anargiroi *Athens (W)* or *AW*	Polidrosso *Athens (M)* or *AM*	Kolonaki *Athens (I)*
Bologna	La Barca *Bologna (W)* or *BW*	Bolognina *Bologna (M)* or *BM*	Centro Storico *Bologna (I)* or *BI*
Dublin	Jobstown *Dublin (W)* or *DW*	Clonskeagh *Dublin (M)* or *DM*	North Docklands *Dublin (I)* or *DI*
Helsinki	Kontula *Helsinki (I)* or *HI*	Länsi-Pakila *Helsinki (M)* or *HM*	Taka- Töölö *Helsinki (I)* or *HI*

The ethnographic study was designed by the Dublin team and the sampling methodology for the survey by the Greek team; the focus group element was designed and co-ordinated by the Finnish team. This triangulation of methods ensured that in each area we had usually two and often three sources of information on different issues. The data and the choice of localities allow the *double contextualisation* of mobility in general (and of car usage in particular) in terms of both the city and the locality.

The final stage of the research returned to the level of the case study city. In each city we invited city policy makers and transport experts to a scenario-building exercise. We asked participants to discuss how they would *like* the city to be ('desired scenario') in the future and how they would *expect* the city to be ('expected scenario'). Similarly, we asked them which transport technologies (e.g. trams, road pricing) they hoped to see used in their city in the future, and which technologies they expected to see used. On this basis, we drew up plausible mobility scenarios for each city.

The research began in 1998 and was completed in 2000; final reports were submitted in 2002. The full research reports from the project are available from the project website (http://www.tcd.ie/erc/pastprojectcars.php) which also lists all publications based on the research. An academic monograph study of all four cities will be published in 2006.

Bibliography

Albert, D., 'Psychotechnology and Insanity at the Wheel', Journal of the History of the Behavioural Sciences 35 (3), 1999, pp. 291-305

Apel, D. and T. Pharaoh, Transport Concepts in European Cities, Aldershot, Avebury, 1995

Atkinson, A. et al, Social Indicators: The EU and social inclusion, Oxford UP

Baker, M.H.C., Irish Railways since 1916, London, Ian Allan, 1972

Barrett, S., Transport Policy in Ireland in the 1990s, Dublin, Gill and Macmillan, 1991

Betz, H. G., Right-Wing Populism in Europe, London, Macmillan, 1994

Blakely, E. and M.G. Snyder, Fortress America: Gated Communities in the United States, Washington DC, Brookings Institute, 1997

Boucher, G., C. Conway and E. van der Meer, 'Tiers of Engagement by Universities in their Region's Development', Regional Studies 37(9), 2003, pp. 887-897

Bratzel, S., Extreme der Mobilität: Entwicklung und Folgen der Verkehrspolitik in Los Angeles, Basel, Birkhäuser Verlag, 1995

Breathnach, P. 'Globalisation, information technology and the emergence of niche transnational cities', Geoforum 31, 2000, pp. 477-485

Brown, P. and R. Scase, Higher education and corporate realities: Class, culture and the decline of graduate careers, London, UCL, 1994

Cevero, R. and C. Radisch, 'Travel choices in pedestrian versus automobile oriented neighbourhoods', *Transport Policy* 3(3), 1996. pp. 127-141

Connor, S., 'US climate policy bigger threat to world than terrorism', *Independent*, 9 January 2004

Cooper, J., T. Ryley and A. Smyth, (2001). 'Contemporary lifestyles...and sustainable development policy: lessons from the UK's most car dependent city, Belfast', *Cities* 18(2), 2001, pp. 103-113

Craig, M., *Dublin 1660-1860: a social and architectural history*, London, CressetP, 1980 (first published 1952)

Crouch, C., D. Finegold and M. Sako, *Are Skills the Answer? The political economy of skill creation in advanced societies*, Oxford UP (paperback edition), 2001

CSO – Central Statistics Office, *Vehicle Registrations 2005*, Cork, Central Statistics Office, 2006

Davis, R., *Death on the Streets: Cars and the mythology of road safety*, UK, Leading Edge Press, 1992/3

de Bellaigue, C. , 'The Persian Difference', *New York Review of Books*, 52(20), 15 December 2005, pp. 16-20

Department of Public Enterprise, *A New Institutional and Regulatory Framework for Public Transport*, Dublin, Stationery Office, 2000

Department of the Environment and Local Government and the Department of Public Enterprise, *New Institutional Arrangements for Land Use and Transport in the Greater Dublin Area*, Dublin, Stationery Office, 2001

Department of the Environment, *National Climate Strategy Ireland*, Dublin, Department of the Environment, 2000

Doherty, M., *'Does the Union Still Make Us Strong? Trade Union Membership in the Partnership Era'*, ongoing doctoral thesis, Trinity College Dublin (2006)

Doyle, D., 'In praise of two lines that serve as a monument to modernity', *Sunday Tribune* 26 June 2005

Drudy, P.J. and M. Punch, *Out of Reach: Inequalities in the Irish housing system*, Dublin, Tasc at New Island, 2005

DTO – Dublin Transportation Office, *A Platform for Change: Outline of an integrated transportation strategy for the Greater Dublin Area 2000 to 2016*, Dublin, Dublin Transportation Office, 2000

DTO – Dublin Transportation Office, *Annual Report 2002*, Dublin, DTO, 2003

DTO – Dublin Transportation Office, *Road User Monitoring Report 2005*, Dublin, DTO

Duany, A., E. Plater-Zyberk and J. Speck, *Suburban Nation: The rise of sprawl and the decline of the American dream*, NY, North Point Press, 2001

Dublin Bus, *Bus Átha Cliath: Annual Report and Financial Statements 2002*, Dublin, Dublin Bus, 2003

Dublin City Council, *Air Quality and Noise Control Unit, Annual Report 2002-2003*, Dublin, Dublin City Council, 2003

ECMT – European Conference of Ministers of Transport, *Transport Policy and the Environment*, Paris, ECMT in association with OECD, 1990

EPA – Environmental Protection Agency, *Ireland's Environment*, Wexford, EPA, 2004

Erskine, A., 'The Burden of Risk: Who dies because of cars?' *Social Policy and Administration* 30(2), 1996, pp. 143-157

European Commission, *Green Paper: Promoting healthy diets and physical activity*, Brussels, European Commission COM2005/637 final, 2005

Fine-Davis, M., *Fathers and mothers: Dilemmas of the work life balance. A comparative study in four European Countries*, Dordrecht, Boston and London, Kluwer Academic, 2004

Fischer-Kowalski, M. and C. Amann, 'Beyond IPAT and Kuznets curves: globalization as a vital factor in analysing the environmental impact of socio-economic metabolism', *Population and Environment* 23(1), 2001, pp. 7-47

Frank, L. D. et al. 'Obesity Relationships with Community

design, physical activity and time spent in cars', *American Journal of Preventive Medicine* 27(2), 2004, pp. 87-96

Freund, P. and G. Martin, *The Ecology of the Automobile*, Montreal, Black Rose Press, 1993

Friedl, B. and M. Getzner, 'Determinants of CO2 emissions in a small open economy', *Ecological Economics* 45(1), 2003, pp. 133-148

Garreau, J., *Edge City: Life on the new frontier*, Garden City, NY, Doubleday, 1991

GomezIbanez, J.A. and J.R. Meyer, 'Alternatives for urban bus services: An international perspective on the British reforms', *Transport Reviews* 17(1), 1997, pp. 17-29

Gramsci, A., *Selections from the prison notebooks of Antonio Gramsci*, London, Lawrence and Wishart, 1971

Haberl, H., 'Progress towards sustainability? What the conceptual framework of material and energy flow accounting (MEFA) can offer', *Land Use Policy* 21 (3), 2004, pp. 199-213

Hajer, M.A. et al. *The Politics of Environmental Discourse*, Oxford UP, 1997

Hodge, D. C., 'My fair share: equity issues in urban transport' in S. Hanson (ed.), *The Geography of Urban Transportation*, NY/London, Guilford Press, 1995, pp. 359-375

Hunt, T., *Building Jerusalem: The rise and fall of the Victorian City*, London, Weidenfeld & Nicholson, 2004

Hutton, W., *The World We're In*, London, Little, Brown, 2002

Jacobs, J., *The Death and Life of Great American Cities*, London, Jonathan Cape, 1962

Jacobson, D., 'The political economy of industrial location: the Ford Motor Company at Cork, 1912-1926', *Irish Economic and Social History* 4, 1977, pp. 36-55

Jaggi, M. et al, *Red Bologna*, London, Pluto, 1977

Jenks, M., 'Above and below the line: Globalization and urban form in Bangkok', *Annals of Regional Science* 37, 2003, pp. 547-557

Joseph, S., *Bringing Buses Up To Standard*, London, Transport 2000 (Policy paper), 2002

Judt, T., *Postwar: A history of Europe since 1945*, London, William Heinemann, 2005

Katz, P. (ed.), *The New Urbanism: Towards an Architecture of Community*, NY, McGraw-Hill, 1994

Kaufmann, V., *Rethinking mobility: Contemporary sociology*, Aldershot, Ashgate, 2002

Kay, J., 'The balance sheet' [Twenty years of privatisation], *Prospect*, No. 76, 2002, pp. 22-28

Kennedy, D., 'London bus tendering: a welfare balance', *Transport Policy* 2(4), 1995, pp. 243-249

Kenworthy, J., 'Automobile dependence in Bangkok: an international comparison with implications for planning policies', *World Transport Policy & Practice* 1(3), 1995, pp. 31-41

Kenworthy, J., F. Laube, P. Newman and P. Barter, *Indicators of Transport Efficiency in 37 Global Cities. A Report for the World Bank*, Perth (Aus), Murdock University, Sustainable Transport Research Group, 1997

Killen, J., 'Transport in Dublin: past, present and future' in F. Aalen and K. Whelan (eds) *Dublin city and county*, Dublin, Geography Publications, 1992, pp. 305-325

Kowinski, W. S., *The Malling of America: An Inside Look at the Great Consumer Paradise*, NY, William Morrow, 1985

Kunstler, J.H., *Home from Nowhere: Remaking Our Everyday World for the Twenty-First Century*, NY, Simon & Schuster, 1996

Lang, R.E. and K.A. Danielson, 'Gated communities in America: walling out the world?' *Housing Policy Debate* 8(4), 1997, pp. 867-877

Lohan, M., 'Dublin' in J. Wickham (ed.) *The Car System in the City*, SceneSusTech Report, Dublin, ERC, 1999

Luymes, D., 'The fortification of suburbia', *Landscape & Urban Plannning*, 39, 1997, pp. 187-203

MacLaran, A. and J. Killen, 'The Suburbanisation of Office

Development in Dublin and its Transport Implications', *Journal of Irish Urban Studies* 1(1), 2002, pp. 21-35

MacLaran, A., 'Inner Dublin: Change and Development' in J. Killen and A. MacLaran (eds) *Dublin, Contemporary Trends*, 1999, pp. 21-33

Marshall, A., 'European Regional Policy and Urban Governance: Assessing Dublin's Experience', ECPR conference, Turin, 2002

Marshall, T.H., *Citizenship and Social Class and Other Essays*, Cambridge, Cambridge UP, 1950

McDonald, F., *The Construction of Dublin*, Kinsale, Gandon Editions, 2000

McDonald, F. and J. Nix, *Chaos at the Crossroads*, Kinsale, Gandon Books, 2005

McManus, R., *Dublin, 1910–40: Shaping the City and Suburbs*, Dublin, Four Courts Press, 2002

Mingione, E., 'Urban Poverty in the Advanced Industrial World: Concepts, Analysis and Debates' in E. Mingione (ed.) *Urban Poverty and the Underclass*, Oxford, Blackwell, 1996, pp. 3-40

Murray, A., *Off the Rails*, London, Verso, 2001

National Audit Office, *Improving public transport in England through light rail*, London, The Stationery Office, 2004

National Taskforce on Obesity, *Obesity: The Policy Challenges: Report of the National Taskforce*, Dublin, Department of Health and Children, 2005

NERA and TIS.PT, *Models for the provision, regulation and integration of public transport services*, London, National Economic Research Associates (Final Report for the Public Transport Partnership Forum), 2001

Newman, P.W.G. and J.R. Kenworthy, 'The land use-transport connection – An overview', *Land Use Policy* 13(1), 1996, pp. 1-22

Nijkamp, P., S. Rienstra, and J. Vleugel, *Transportation, Planning and the Future*, Chichester, John Wiley & Sons, 1998

Nolan, B., C. Whelan and J. Williams, 'Spatial Aspects of Poverty and Deprivation in Ireland' in D. Pringle (ed.) *Poor People, Poor Places,* Dublin, Oak Tree Press, 1999, pp. 37-74

OECD, *Pollution Prevention and Control. Environmental criteria for sustainable transport,* Paris, OECD (Report on Phase 1 of the project on environmentally sustainable transport, EST), 1996

Olsthoorn, X., 'Implications of Globalization for CO2 Emissions from Transport', *Transportation and Planning* 26(1), 2003, pp. 105-133

Østby, P., 'Escape from Detroit - The Norwegian Conquest of an alien artifact' in K. Sorenson (ed.) *The Car and its Environments,* Brussels, European Commission COST Programme, 1994, pp. 33-68

Peillon, M., M. Corcoran and J. Gray, *Civic Engagement and the Governance of Irish Suburbs,* Dublin, Policy Institute, 2006

Peltzman, S., 'The Effects of automobile safety regulation', *Journal of Political Economy* 83(4), 1975, pp. 677-725

Poboon, C., *Anatomy of a Traffic Disaster: Towards a Sustainable Solution to Bangkok's Traffic Problems,* Murdoch University, Murdoch, Western Australia, PhD dissertation, 1997

Pucher, J., 'Urban transport in Germany: Providing feasible alternatives to the car', *Transport Review* 18 (4), 1998, pp. 285-310

Pucher, J. and S. Kurth, 'Verkehrsverbund: the success of regional public transport in Germany', *Transport Policy* 2(4), 1996, pp. 279-291

Putnam, R. D., *Bowling Alone: The collapse and revival of American community,* NY, Simon & Schuster, 2000

Rajanti, M., 'Local Mobility Experience in its social context: focus group results' in J. Wickham (ed.) *Scenarios for a sustainable society ... final report of project SceneSusTech,* Dublin, Employment Research Centre, 2002, http://www.tcd.ie/erc/oldprojectcars.php

Rogers, R., *Cities for a small planet*, London, Faber & Faber, 1997

Sallis, J. F. et al., 'Active transportation and physical activity: opportunities for collaboration on transportation and health research', *Transportation Research Part A* 38, 2004, pp. 249-268

Sennett, R., *The Fall of Public Man*, London, Penguin (first published NY, 1977), 2002

Simms, A., *Ghost Town Britain*, London, New Economics Foundation, 2002, URL: http://www.neweconomics .org.

Sorensen, K. H. and J. Sorgaard, 'Modernity and Mobility: Towards a Sociology of Cars' in K. Sorensen (ed.), *The Car and its environments*, 1994, Brussels, European Commission (COST programme), pp. 1-32

Stokes, G., 'Alternative Strategies to Reduce Car Dependence', CAPTURE Conference Cities Conference, Institute of Civil Engineers, London, 9 December 1996

TEST, *Wrong side of the tracks? Impacts of road rail transport on the environment: a basis for discussion*, London, TEST, 1991

Tfl – Transport for London, *The case for investing in London's buses – Presenting the results of the London Buses Strategic Review*, London, TfL, 2003

Thomson, R. et al, 'Choice, chance and opportunity in young people's narratives of transition', *Sociology* 36(2), 2002, pp. 335-374

Townsend, P., *Poverty in the United Kingdom: A survey of household resources and standards of living*, Harmondsworth, Penguin, 1979

Urry, J., 'Mobility and Proximity', *Sociology* 36(2), 2002, pp. 225-274

van Egerat, C., M. Sokol and P. Stafford, 'Greater Dublin the Celtic Tiger Economy: Towards a polycentric mega-city region?' in P. Hall and K. Pain (eds) *The Polycentric Metropolis: Learning from Mega-City-Regions in Europe*,

London, Earthscan/James & James (forthcoming) 2006

Webster, J. et al, *Innovations in Information Society Service Sectors: Implications for women's work, expertise and opportunities in European workplaces*, Final Report of the SERVEMPLOI project, Dublin, Employment Research Centre, 2002

Whitelegg, J., *Transport for a sustainable future: the case for Europe*, London, Belhaven Press, 1993

Wickham, J., *The End of the European Social Model – Before it Began?* Dublin, Employment Research Centre, Trinity College Dublin, 2002

Wickham, J. et al., *Scenarios for a sustainable society: Car transport and the sociology of embedded technologies. Final report of Project SceneSusTech.* Dublin, Employment Research Centre, report for European Commission, 2002 http://www.tcd.ie/erc/oldprojectcars.php

Wickham, J., 'Changing Times: Working time in Ireland 1983-2000,' Dublin, Employment Research Centre Labour Market Observatory, 2000 http://www.tcd.ie/erc/observatory.php

Wickham, J., 'Public transport systems: the sinews of European urban citizenship?' *European Societies,* 8(1), 2006, pp. 3-26

Williams, B. and P. Shiels, 'The Expansion of Dublin and the Policy Implications of Dispersal', *Irish Journal of Urban Studies* 1(1), 2002, pp. 1-19

Wolf, W., *Car Mania: A critical history of transport*, London Pluto, 1996

Wolmar, C., *Stagecoach: A classic rags-to-riches tale from the frontiers of capitalism*, London, Orion Publishing, 1999

Wolmar, C., *Broken Rails: How Privatisation Wrecked Britain's Railways*, UK: Aurum, 2001

Wolmar, C., Down the Tube: The battle for London's Underground, London, Aurum Press, 2002

Yago, G., *The Decline of Transit: Urban transportation in German and US cities 1900-1970*, Cambridge: Mass, Cambridge UP, 1984

Index

December 2005

Out of Reach
Inequalities in the Irish Housing System

by **PJ Drudy and Michael Punch**

How is it possible that Ireland, now one of the richest countries in the European Union, has a serious housing crisis?

Why have house prices risen beyond the reach of so many? Why are standards of accommodation and insecurity in the private rented sector a persistent problem for tenants? Why has the provision of social housing fallen so far short of requirements at a time of massive housing need and a growing homeless population? Why do we continue to sell off Local Authority housing to tenants and public land to private developers? Is the current enthusiasm for public private partnerships justified?

And what has government done to deal with the housing crisis?

P.J. Drudy and Michael Punch set out to answer these questions. Is it acceptable that housing should be treated as yet another commodity to be traded on the 'market' like race horses, motor cars or stocks and shares? Or should housing be treated as a shelter and a home – a not-for-profit necessity and a right to be achieved by all, irrespective of ability to pay?

The authors propose a number of central principles and policy innovations for a more progressive and equitable housing system.

October 2005

The Report of the Democracy Commission

Engaging Citizens

The Case for Democratic Renewal in Ireland

Edited by **Clodagh Harris**

David Begg,
Ivana Bacik, Ruth Barrington, John Hanafin, Bernadette MacMahon,
Elizabeth Meehan, Nora Owen, Donal Toolan, Tony Kennedy, Mark
Mortell, Caroline Wilson

'We think we have come as close as is possible to getting a clear picture of the health of democracy in both parts of Ireland. We hope that our conclusions will, in the course of time, strengthen democracy on the island of Ireland and support those who make it work.' David Begg.

Establishing the Commission was the initiative of two think tanks, TASC in Dublin and Democratic Dialogue in Belfast. Launched in 2003 the Commission was asked to enquire into the causes of disconnection for large groups of people from even the most basic forms of democratic participation in decision-making. The members of the independent commission, acting in a voluntary capacity, made public engagement the cornerstone of their work.

The report of the Commission has been described as a really excellent and thought provoking document on all the fronts it addresses. It draws on - and directs readers to - recent research in all areas, and yet is really accessible'

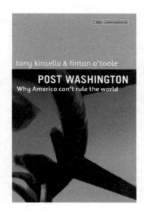

June 2005

Post Washington
Why America can't rule the world

by **Tony Kinsella and Fintan O'Toole**

Has the American Dream been replaced by the American myth?

The United States is the largest military, economic and cultural power in history. The aspirational focus of billions, the US leads the world into a brighter tomorrow, a tomorrow modelled exclusively on its own achievements. Our future lies in a US Imperium.

But, just as the sun sets on a *Pax Brittanica*, has it yet to even rise on a *Pax Americana?* Here writer and commentator Tony Kinsella and Irish Times' journalist and author Fintan O'Toole, argue that the United States of America is not only incapable of maintaining its dominant position in the world, but that this dominance is, at the very least, exaggerated and over-estimated.

Post Washington argues that the US system cannot continue. An extraordinary fragile economy straddles an agricultural sector on the verge of disaster, while the level of public and private debt threatens to topple a social and political structure crying out for reform.

At the dawn of the 21st century, the greatest threat to America comes from within. 'The world cannot wait for the US to wake from its slumber', say the authors. 'We must move on, building our post-Washington world- with the US where possible, but without it where necessary.'

May 2005

For Richer, For Poorer
An investigation into the Irish
Pension System

edited by Jim Stewart

With current pension policy widening income inequality in Irish society, a large proportion of our pensioners, particularly women, will be without adequate income in their old age.

For Richer, For Poorer sets out a radical and revised criteria for our pension system, outlining key proposals on what should constitute a pension strategy for Ireland.

Provocative and timely, *For Richer, For Poorer* argues that our current system is skewed towards the better off. Exposing a system that has evolved to serve the interests of the pension industry, the book offers both a critical evaluation of this system and makes clear policy recommendations.

With Peter Connell on demographics; Gerard Hughes on the cost of tax expenditures; Tony McCashin on the State Social security system; Jim Stewart on sources of income to the retired population, Sue Ward on the UK pension system, *For Richer, For Poorer* explores the problems with the current system, and recommends that while the UK has been our guide, it should not be our model.

November 2004

An Outburst of Frankness
Community arts in Ireland –
a Reader

edited by **Sandy Fitzgerald**

An Outburst of Frankness is the first serious attempt to gather together a wide range of views dealing with the history, theory and practice of community arts in Ireland. Not an academic book, the style, over twelve commissioned essays and the edited transcripts of two unique fora, is accessible and open, ranging from a general art-history perspective to the particular experiences of artists working in and with communities.

Besides the politics, the rhetoric and the debates, there are values around this activity called community arts which are as relevant today as they were forty or four hundred years ago. At the core of these values is the question of power and the right of people to contribute to and participate fully in culture; the right to have a voice and the right to give voice. From this point of view, arts and culture should be at the centre of all political, social, educational, individual and communal activity, particularly in this time of unprecedented and sometimes dangerous change, for Ireland and the world.

October 2004

Selling Out?
Privatisation in Ireland

by **Paul Sweeney**

This is the story of privatisation in Ireland – who made money, who lost money and whether the taxpayer gained. It sets the limits on privatisation – what should not be sold for money – and it shows that privatisation is about not only ownership but also public influence and control. It proves that this government has already sold out key assets, that consumers now pay higher prices and competitiveness has been lost. Examining the story of the Eircom privatisation, Sweeney shows how this triumph for 'popular capitalism' was, in fact, a hard lesson in why some state assets should never be privatised.

Sweeney quantifies the billions in gains made by the state on its investments in the state companies and how much the remaining companies are worth, and he proposes reforms to dynamise the remaining state companies to the advantage of the taxpayer, the consumer, society and the economy.

October 2003

After the Ball

by Fintan O'Toole

Is it the death of communal values? Or the triumph of profit? In a series of sharply observed essays, Fintan O'Toole the award-winning *Irish Times* commentator, looks at Ireland's growing notoriety as one of the most globalised yet unequal economies on earth. Why were the boom years haunted by the spectre of a failing health service? Why do a substantial proportion of our children continue to be marginalised through lack of funding in education? What is the place of people with disabilities, travellers, women immigrants and asylum-seekers in our brave new land?

Passionate and provocative, *After the Ball* is a wake-up call for a nation in transition. Irish people like to see Ireland as a exceptional place. In this starting polemic, Fintan O'Toole shatters the illusion once and for all.

Support TASC
A Think Tank for Action on Social Change.

> *'the limited development of think tanks is a striking feature [of Ireland]*
> *for such bodies could do much to focus new thinking about the country's*
> *future democratic and political development'*

(REPORT TO THE
JOSEPH ROWNTREE CHARITABLE TRUST, 2002)

Ireland almost uniquely in Europe has relatively few think tanks of any kind and, prior to the establishment of TASC, none whose sole agenda is to foster new thinking on ways to create a more progressive and equal society.

Your support is essential – to do its work TASC must keep a distance from political and monetary pressure in order to protect the independence of its agenda. If you would like to make a contribution to TASC – A Think Tank for Action on Social Change, please send your donation to the address below

DONATIONS TO:
TASC
A Think Tank for Action on Social Change
26 Sth Frederick St, Dublin 2.
Ph: 00353 1 6169050
Email:contact@tascnet.ie
www.tascnet.ie